ADVERTISING

Maria Townsley

SOUTH-WESTERN
THOMSON LEARNING

Australia • Canada • Mexico • Singapore • Spain • United Kingdom • United States

Business 2000
Advertising
by Maria Townsley

Executive Editor
Eve Lewis

Project Manager
Enid Nagel

Production Manager
Patricia Matthews Boies

Marketing Manager
Nancy A. Long

Marketing Coordinator
Chris L. McNamee

Editor
Colleen A. Farmer

Print Buyer
Kevin L. Kluck

Cover and Internal Design
Bill Spencer

Team Assistant
Linda Adams

Editorial Assistant
Stephanie L. White

Compositor
New England Typographic Services

Printer
Banta Company, Menasha

About the Author
Maria Townsley has been an educator and a professional writer in the business and educational arenas since 1984. Her corporate business activities include creating marketing materials and designing and implementing software documentation and training courses. Active in adult education and business training programs, Ms. Townsley has been a member of the Society for Technical Communication for many years.

ISBN: 0-538-69870-5

Annotated Instructor's Edition
ISBN: 0-538-69874-8

Printed in the United States of America
1 2 3 4 5 6 BM 05 04 03 02 01 00

For permission to use material from this text or product, contact us by

Tel: 800-730-2214
Fax: 800-730-2215
Web: www.thomsonrights.com

For more information, contact South-Western Educational Publishing, 5101 Madison Road, Cincinnati, OH, 45227-1490. Or you can visit our Internet site at

www.swep.com

International Divisions List

Asia (including India)
Thomson Learning
60 Albert Street, #15-01
Albert Complex
Singapore 189969
Tel 65 336-6411
Fax 65 336-7411

Australia/New Zealand
Nelson
102 Dobbs Street
South Melbourne
Victoria 3205
Australia
Tel 61 (0)3 9685-4111
Fax 61 (0)3 9685-4199

Canada
Nelson
1120 Birchmount Road
Toronto, Ontario
Canada M1K 5G4
Tel (416) 752-9100
Fax (416) 752-8102

Latin America
Thomson Learning
Seneca 53
Colonia Polanco
11560 Mexico, D.F. Mexico
Tel (525) 281-2906
Fax (525) 281-2656

Spain (including Portugal)
Paraninfo
Calle Magallanes 25
28015 Madrid
Espana
Tel 34 (0)91 446-3350
Fax 34 (0)91 445-6218

UK/Europe/Middle East/Africa
Thomson Learning
Berkshire House
168-173 High Holborn
London WC 1V 7AA
United Kingdom
Tel 44 (0)20 497-1422
Fax 44 (0)20 497-1426

YOUR COURSE PLANNING JUST GOT EASIER!

NEW! Business 2000 is an exciting new modular instructional program that allows you to create customized courses or enhance already existing curriculum.

BUSINESS 2000

Intro to Business by Robert A. Ristau
0-538-69865-9 Learner Guide
0-538-69866-7 Module*
0-538-69869-1 Annotated Instructor's Edition

Entrepreneurship by Cynthia L. Greene
0-538-69875-6 Learner Guide
0-538-69876-4 Module*
0-538-69879-9 Annotated Instructor's Edition

Advertising by Maria Townsley
0-538-69870-5 Learner Guide
0-538-69871-3 Module*
0-538-69874-8 Annotated Instructor's Edition

E-Commerce by Dotty Boen Oelkers
0-538-69880-2 Learner Guide
0-538-69881-0 Module*
0-538-69884-5 Annotated Instructor's Edition

****Each module includes one Learner Guide, Video, Annotated Instructor's Edition, and Instructor's CD.***

NEW! ***International Business*** by Dlabay and Scott
This hardbound text provides the foundation for studying international business and the many aspects of conducting business in the global economy. Semester or year-long course.

0-538-69855-1 Student Edition
0-538-69857-8 Student Activities Study Guide
0-538-69858-6 Printed Tests
0-538-69859-4 Video

NEW! ***Business Principles and Management*** by Everard and Burrow
The eleventh edition of the market-leading text presents the sound fundamental topics needed to manage and operate a successful business. Semester or year-long course.

0-538-69793-8 Student Edition
0-538-69892-6 Student Workbook
0-538-69894-2 Student CD
0-538-69893-4 Printed Tests
0-538-69891-8 Video Package

NEW! SCANS 2000 Virtual Workplace Simulations in partnership with Johns Hopkins University
These CDs create a challenging, interactive workplace experience that gives learners a chance to develop and apply their academic and soft skills in a real-world setting.

0-538-69827-6 Developing a Business Plan
0-538-69819-5 Developing a Marketing Plan
0-538-69811-X Building a Problem Solving Team

NEW! ***Investing in Your Future*** by NAIC
This text-workbook can teach learners every step of the way toward smart saving and investing. 30+ hours completion time.

0-538-68607-3 Student Edition (includes Stock Selection Guide Software CD)

NEW! ***Sports and Entertainment Marketing*** by Kaser and Oelkers
This text-workbook takes your student on a step-by-step journey through the world of marketing.

0-538-69477-7 Student Edition
0-538-69479-3 Annotated Teacher's Edition
0-538-69478-5 Module (includes Student Edition, Annotated Teacher's Edition, and CD-ROM)

Join Us on the Internet **www.swep.com**

HOW TO USE THIS BOOK
ENGAGE STUDENT INTEREST

CAREERS IN ADVERTISING
Highlights a real-world company and how it uses advertising.

LESSONS
Make the text easy to use in all classroom environments.

VIDEO
Contains clips from several resources that can be used to introduce concepts in each chapter.

VIDEO
The Chapter 5 video for this module introduces the concepts in this chapter.

PROJECT
Group or individual activity that has activities for each lesson.

PROJECT

Create Advertisements

PROJECT OBJECTIVES

- Select a message strategy that can be used in different media
- Create an integrated advertising campaign using print and television advertisements

GETTING STARTED

Read through the Project Process below. Make a list of any materials you will need. Decide how you will get the needed materials or information.

- The Running Shoe specializes in shoes for runners. The owner is a long-distance runner who usually finishes in one of the top five positions in local marathon and minimarathon races. She is well known among local runners. The Running Shoe is small but has become very profitable since the owner opened a catalog service five years ago, then branched to Internet sales two years ago.
- Look in newspapers and magazines for advertisements for related fields such as sports equipment and running shoe stores. Bring in the advertisements. Look on the Internet for banner ads relating to sports equipment and running shoes. Bring in printouts of the banner ads you find.

PROJECT PROCESS

Part 1 **LESSON 5.1** Select a message strategy that will be effective for the business. Write a slogan for the business.
Part 2 **LESSON 5.2** Fill in the components of the creative plan by determining the target segment, advertising message, and so on.
Part 3 **LESSON 5.3** Create a print advertisement for a newspaper or magazine using the creative plan.
Part 4 **LESSON 5.4** Create a storyboard for a television commercial that carries the same advertising message.

CHAPTER REVIEW

Project Wrap-up Draw the print advertisement and storyboard for the television commercial. Present them to the class. Be prepared to perform the television commercial.

CHAPTER 5 CREATE YOUR ADVERTISEMENT

LESSON 5.1
SELECT A STRATEGY

GOALS
Begin each lesson and offer an overview.

GOALS

PREPARE advertising messages driven by the product

PREPARE advertising messages driven by the user

BASE YOUR ADVERTISING MESSAGE ON THE PRODUCT

Advertisers want to capture your attention when you are doing something else. You do not drive down the street, flip through a magazine, or watch television hoping to see an advertisement. You are there for some other reason. You are trying to get somewhere, read an interesting article, or watch a television program.

Advertisers have only seconds to distract you from your main purpose. Once an advertisement has distracted you, it must keep your attention and deliver a message. This message strategy, the advertiser's objectives and the methods used to carry out the objectives, is a key component of the advertising plan. Objectives are based on attributes of the product or the user.

ON THE SCENE

Ling Jen owns a chain of 50 jewelry stores throughout the United States. She has come to your agency because she wants to launch an advertising campaign that uses several types of media. She is interested in print, radio, and television advertisements. Right now, she has to decide what type of message strategy she should use. The jewelry is high quality. There are also a small number of custom design orders every year. What type of message strategy would you recommend? What specific message would you create?

104

ON THE SCENE
Lesson opening scenario that provides motivation.

5.1 SELECT A STRATEGY

celebrities, including athletes, actors, and models. They are individuals the consumer might want to imitate. The product does not have to be in the celebrity's area of expertise. Athletes recommend athletic shoes and golf clubs, but they also recommend coffee makers and investment firms.

People with recognized experience in a specific field give *expert testimonials*. Doctors recommend over-the-counter medicines for common medical problems. Master chefs recommend kitchen appliances. Several years ago, in a slight twist to this approach, burglars recommended home security systems and antitheft devices.

An average person who uses a product provides the *average-user testimonial*. This user has no expertise or fame and is just like anyone in the target segment. If the product works well for an average person, it should work for anyone. Average users can recommend almost any product—from trucks to athlete's foot remedies.

Demonstration "Show them. Don't tell them." This old saying is a good principle to follow for visual media such as print and television. "Before" and "after" photographs are used to advertise more than diet products. Vinyl siding, lawn care products, and cleaning services can use the demonstration strategy effectively.

Advertorial Limited to print media, the *advertorial* is a special advertising section in a publication. It is designed to look like an editorial placed in the magazine or newspaper. This type of presentation enables the advertiser to provide more information than an advertisement would normally contain. It also lends credibility because it looks like an editorial, news story, or article, rather than an advertisement.

Infomercial An advertiser buys television airtime to broadcast an advertisement called an *infomercial*. Infomercials are usually 30 minutes long, but can last from 5 to 60 minutes. The infomercial is often presented as a documentary. Hosted by a narrator, the program contains demonstrations and testimonials. Infomercials are usually broadcast during off-peak hours, late at night, or during the day on weekends. A product or service can benefit from this approach if the target segment will be watching at that time.

WORKSHOP

How many slogans and jingles can you remember? Make a list. Can you match those phrases to the associated product? How many of the products do you buy?

WORKSHOP
Provides activities to use in class.

CHECKPOINT

Why is the persuasive strategy difficult?

109

CHECKPOINT
Short questions within lessons to assist with reading and to assure students are grasping concepts.

SPECIAL FEATURES ENHANCE LEARNING

Select a commercial for a familiar product, such as toothpaste or clothing. Identify the format and the message strategy. How would you create a magazine advertisement from the commercial? Draw the advertisement, and explain it to the class.

COMMUNICATE
Provide activities to reinforce, review, and practice communication skills.

BUSINESS MATH CONNECTION
Worked example that reinforces and reviews math concepts.

BUSINESS MATH CONNECTION

There were 1,408,041 bankruptcy filings in 1998. In 1990, that number was 718,107. Calculate the percent of increase in bankruptcy filings between 1990 and 1998.

SOLUTION

To determine the percent of increase, first subtract the number of 1990 filings from the number of 1999 filings. Then, divide the result by the number of 1990 filings.

$$\frac{\text{1999 Filings} - \text{1990 Filings}}{\text{1990 Filings}} =$$

$$\frac{1{,}408{,}041 - 718{,}107}{718{,}107} = 0.96\text{, or } 96\%$$

Bankruptcy filings increased by 96% from 1990 to 1998.

DID YOU KNOW?
Provides an interesting fact about the topic.

A large amount of information about a company, its products, and its competition is available on the Internet. Many companies' web sites also have a copy of their most recent annual report that you can read or download.

TECH TALK
Provides information about new technology that is being used in business.

TECH TALK

COMPUTERS AND ADVERTISING The first television commercial with computer-generated footage was created in 1968. The *Star Wars* feature film was released in 1977, but computer-generated effects were not yet common for television. By 1979, computer-generated commercials were released, including Volkswagen, Chevrolet, and "Live From Lincoln Center." In 1991, PIXAR created ads for Listerine, Life Savers, and Tropicana that set a new standard for broadcast excellence. In 1993, computer graphics took a giant leap forward in the film *Jurassic Park.* Within a few years, the same technology was found in television commercials as well.

THINK CRITICALLY Why is the newest technology used for television commercials?

Dedicated web site b2000.swep.com that provides activities and links for each chapter.

WORLD VIEW
Provides international business connections relevant to today's current events.

WORLD VIEW

ADVERTISING IN CHINA

Many experts believe that the Chinese economy will grow about 9 percent every year. In cities, retail sales rose 25 percent each year from 1995 to 1997. As the average Chinese income rises, China will continue to be an important consumer market.

China's advertising market has been marked as the eighth largest in the world. Advertising spending in 1996 was estimated at $3.9 billion. As new brands and products are introduced, retailers face competition in the market. The advertising market has room for growth, providing opportunity for American companies hoping to expand into the Chinese market. A 1996 survey showed that advertising in China averaged $3 per person. Advertising in America for the same time period averaged $330 per person.

THINK CRITICALLY What factors make the Chinese market attractive to U.S. retailers? What role will advertising play?

ASSESSMENT AND REVIEW

THINK CRITICALLY

1. What is the difference between a need and a want?
2. What are the two types of benefits consumers want in the products they buy?
3. What is an example of consumer behavior?
4. Which type of advertising should you ignore? Explain.
5. Can a poor product succeed if it is well advertised?

MAKE CONNECTIONS

6. COMMUNICATION Amelia Sturling is sitting in her new art gallery waiting for customers to find her. Write her a one-page recommendation of things she could do to make customers come to her.
7. RESEARCH Using the library or Internet, determine the amount of money a large company spent on marketing or advertising. Prepare a presentation about your findings.

END-OF-LESSON ACTIVITIES

Think Critically Provides opportunities to apply concepts.

Make Connections Provides connections to other disciplines.

Presentation Icon indicates opportunity to use presentation software, such as PowerPoint.

Word Processing Icon indicates opportunity to use word processing software.

Spreadsheet Icon indicates opportunity to use spreadsheet software.

Internet Icon indicates opportunity to research on the web.

CHAPTER REVIEW

Contains Chapter Summary, Vocabulary Builder, Review Concepts, Apply What You Learned, Make Connections

REVIEW

CHAPTER SUMMARY

LESSON 1.1 Needs and Wants

A. Your purchases are based on your needs and wants. A need is something you can't live without, and a want is something you can live without. It is very important to know the difference between a need and a want when evaluating advertising.

B. Each type of advertising is designed to influence your needs and wants in a different way.

LESSON 1.2 The Consumer Is in Charge

A. Advertising reflects your priorities and values. Sometimes advertising presents an idealized version of life, rather than a realistic one.

B. There are many advantages and disadvantages to advertising that impact you and your society. Among the advantages of advertising are that it provides product information and it makes products cheaper. Among the disadvantages of advertising are that ads can be more biased than informative and it can make products more expensive.

LESSON 1.3 Advertising and the Economy

A. Advertising is an important part of the marketing process. It is a message that must be paid for, must be delivered by mass media, and must try to persuade the audience to do or believe something.

B. Advertising affects the local, national, and global economies. Advertising can be used to help stimulate demand during economic downturns.

VOCABULARY BUILDER

Choose the term that best fits the definition. Write the letter of the answer in the space provided. Some terms may not be used.

____ 1. The minimum level of necessities and luxuries required to maintain an individual or a group at a common level of comfort

____ 2. Form of communication designed to reach a large number of people

____ 3. A paid public announcement, usually emphasizing desirable qualities, to persuade you to buy an item or a service

____ 4. Someone who uses goods

____ 5. The amount of time you would spend to find products or services you want

____ 6. Something that you would like to have but can live without

____ 7. Interpretation of a product or service in a social context

____ 8. Everything that affects or is affected by human consumption

____ 9. Something that you can't live without

a. advertisement
b. consumer
c. consumer behavior
d. mass media
e. need
f. search time
g. social meaning
h. society
i. standard of living
j. want

22

REVIEW CONCEPTS

10. How much of their income do Americans spend?
11. What is the difference between a functional benefit and an emotional benefit?

POINT YOUR BROWSER

b2000.swep.com

APPLY WHAT YOU LEARNED

21. How has your culture affected your consumer behavior?
22. Why is it difficult to convert a brand-loyal consumer?

MAKE CONNECTIONS

25. BUSINESS MATH Contact a local radio station. Compare the prices the station charges for advertising at different times during the day. Make a spreadsheet showing this information. What time is the best buy, taking into account the number of listeners at the time?
29. GOVERNMENT Use the library or Internet. Investigate the *Deceptive Mail Prevention and Enforcement Act* that became law on December 12, 1999, and took effect on April 12, 2000. Write a one-page summary of the law.
30. COMMUNICATION Write the lead paragraph of a press release announcing the promotion of Phil Stroud to senior vice president.
32. PROBLEM SOLVING Suppose you work in the marketing department of a major cookie producer. Create a special promotion for customers.

23

THE POWER OF ADVERTISING 2

CHAPTER 2

THE ADVERTISING INDUSTRY 26

ANALYZE YOUR CUSTOMERS 54

PLAN YOUR ADVERTISING CAMPAIGN 78

CREATE YOUR ADVERTISEMENT 102

PLACE YOUR ADVERTISEMENT 134

REVIEWERS

Jean A. Bitner
Marshfield, WI

E. Keith Brewster
Amarillo, TX

Claudia Dargento
Fair Lawn, NJ

Bruce Dickinson
Sioux Falls, SD

Tommy Georgiades, Jr.
Columbus, OH

Carole S. Goldsmith
Fresno, CA

Linda Harrison
Miami, FL

Frederick Nerone, Ph. D.
Naples, FL

Kerri S. Rosenzweig
Richmond, VA

Cassie Santana
Key West, FL

Alan Sheppard
New Albany, IN

Jill K. Thompson
Winterset, IA

CAREERS IN ADVERTISING

UPS

United Parcel Service of America, Inc., was started in 1907 by nineteen-year-old Jim Casey. Before the U.S. Postal Service delivered packages, Casey borrowed $100 to establish his parcel delivery service focused on retail stores. Today customers around the world depend on UPS to deliver 11.5 million packages a day.

UPS believes that its greatest asset is loyal employees. Throughout its history, UPS has practiced its policies of employee ownership and training. The stock is owned primarily by UPS managers and employees.

The position of Internet Advertising Supervisor reflects the company's attitude toward technology. The Internet Advertising Supervisor plans, negotiates, and implements web-based media solutions. This person works on media strategies to refine messages for target audiences. A Bachelor of Arts or Science degree and four years experience in an agency or in direct marketing is required. Knowledge of Internet technologies, web properties, and ad management tools is also required.

THINK CRITICALLY

1. What strategies helped UPS grow over the years?
2. What aspects about the position of Internet Advertising Supervisor sound attractive to you? Why?

THE POWER OF ADVERTISING

LESSONS

The Chapter 1 video for this module introduces the concepts in this chapter.

PROJECT

Advertising for Video Vector

PROJECT OBJECTIVES

- Evaluate different advertising options
- Select appropriate images for an advertisement
- Choose an appropriate advertising option for a new video and video-rental store, Video Vector
- Develop an advertisement as a part of a marketing plan

GETTING STARTED

Read through the Project Process below. Make a list of any materials you will need. Decide how you will get the needed materials or information.

- A new video and video-rental store, Video Vector, wants to choose new advertising. Decide what you want the advertising to accomplish. For example, do you want to beat a competitor in the marketplace? Do you want to inform consumers of your prices and service?
- Bring in ads you have seen in newspapers, in magazines, and on the Internet or television for other video stores. Discuss them in a group. Which ads are effective? What do the images in the ads say to you? Are you in the advertiser's target market?

PROJECT PROCESS

Part 1 **LESSON 1.1** List the types of advertising you could use for Video Vector. Discuss the advantages and disadvantages of each type of advertising. Decide which advertising media you think would be the most effective for your target market.

Part 2 **LESSON 1.2** Brainstorm ideas for the images you want to use in the ad. Keep your target market in mind. For each image, describe why you think the image would be effective. Write the unwritten message that each image portrays.

Part 3 **LESSON 1.3** Describe how the advertisement fits into a marketing strategy. Use a flow chart to help illustrate your plan. Make sure that your marketing strategy is complete.

CHAPTER REVIEW

Project Wrap-up Draw at least one advertisement, and present the advertisement and the marketing strategy. Suppose your "audience" would be Video Vector, the client. Be prepared to discuss the reasons for your choices.

LESSON 1.1

NEEDS AND WANTS

DIFFERENTIATE between a want and a need

EXPLAIN the impact of advertising on your wants and needs

HOW DO YOU KNOW WHAT YOU WANT?

Every morning, as you move through your normal routine, you use things that were bought by you or for you. The shampoo you used, the sweater you wore, the breakfast cereal you ate, and the jacket you grabbed on your way out the door were all *consumer decisions*. A **consumer** is someone who uses products. Consumers choose to buy items that are needs or wants.

WHAT DO YOU NEED?

A **need** is something that you can't live without. Needs include food, clothes, and shelter. You must have enough food to survive. You must have clothes to protect you from cold weather. You must have a home to protect you from the elements, such as rain, snow, or storms. You have to buy or acquire your needs.

ON THE $CENE

Amelia Sturling has opened a small art gallery in the heart of downtown Denver. Her first show has art pieces in various media, including sculptures, paintings in oil and watercolor, and sketches. All the pieces are by local artists. While she waits for customers to find the gallery, she also sells art supplies. She expects that the art supplies will be the main source of income eventually. Unfortunately, her only customers so far have been the artists whose work she has in the show. Are the supplies she sells needs or wants?

A **want** is something that you would like to have but can live without. Wants are anything that goes beyond filling your basic needs. Therefore, wants include items such as a new electronic game system, a television, and roller skates. You don't have to buy everything you want.

How Much Do You Need? You can easily overspend when you confuse what you want with items you really need. Sometimes you may think you are filling a need, but you will buy more than necessary to fill that need. You must have enough food to survive, but that doesn't mean you need dinner at an expensive restaurant. A winter coat is a need, but a coat that costs $50 more because the style is more popular is a want.

What's the Difference? Your ability to tell the difference between a need and a want is an important skill. Like most skills, it can be learned or improved with practice. Before every purchase, ask yourself if the item is a need or a want. If it is a need, does this item do more than fill the need? For example, is it a popular brand of jeans rather than a basic pair of jeans? If it more than fills the need, is it worth the cost difference?

Sometimes the answers to these questions will be easy. You need a winter coat. You don't need a pair of purple ice skates. Other times the answers will be more difficult. You need a winter coat. Do you need the more expensive coat that is in style this winter?

CONSUMER BEHAVIOR

Your purchasing decisions are more complicated than filling your basic needs. You can decide to buy something now or wait until it goes on sale next week. You could decide to buy a different car, not because it's a better car, but because you like the color or the shape better.

What determines the decisions you make as a consumer? **Consumer behavior** is everything that affects or is affected by human consumption. Of course, there isn't a single theory that explains consumer behavior. It is just as complicated as any other type of human behavior. How you act as a consumer is shaped by your experience, your dreams of the future, and your economic level.

What's In It for Me? Consumers look for products that provide some type of benefit to them. Benefits can be *functional* or *emotional*. Functional benefits are the same for everyone. The new kitchen appliance makes a task easier, faster, or more convenient. The car tires last longer, or they are cheaper. The frozen dinner is more nutritional or has larger servings. These benefits can be measured.

Other benefits are more emotional. Products or services can make you feel proud or satisfied. A luxury car can make you feel more glamorous or rich. Buying something for your child can make you feel like a good parent. Emotional benefits won't be the same for every consumer. One person may buy an alarm system for his house because he worries about his wife and children when he travels. Another individual might buy the same alarm system to protect her home business because it's cheaper than a competitive product. It's the same system but purchased for different reasons. The benefit can't be measured as easily.

CONSUMER SPENDING

Every year, Americans spend almost 98 percent of their after-tax income, the amount remaining after taxes are paid. This means that the average American spends $98 out of every $100 earned, leaving only $2 for saving, investing, or rainy-day emergencies. Over the past few decades, consumer spending has increased. Almost every year, people spend more and more of their income. In fact, many people are spending more than they earn. They get loans and use credit cards to buy items that they can't really afford.

Consumer Overspending Overspending can cause serious financial problems. When you spend more money than you earn, you will eventually run out of money. Items you have purchased but can't pay for will have to be given to the store or bank that loaned you the money. Smaller items, such as furniture or electronics, will probably be returned to the store. Larger items, such as land and houses, will probably be given to the bank or financial institution you owe for the item. The bank will sell the land or house to recover some of the money it loaned to you for the original purchase.

One of the last options you have is to declare bankruptcy. Bankruptcy is a legal condition that remains on your financial record for years. It will have a long-term impact on your future financial activities. As the chart below shows, the number of individuals filing for bankruptcy doubled in the 1990s.

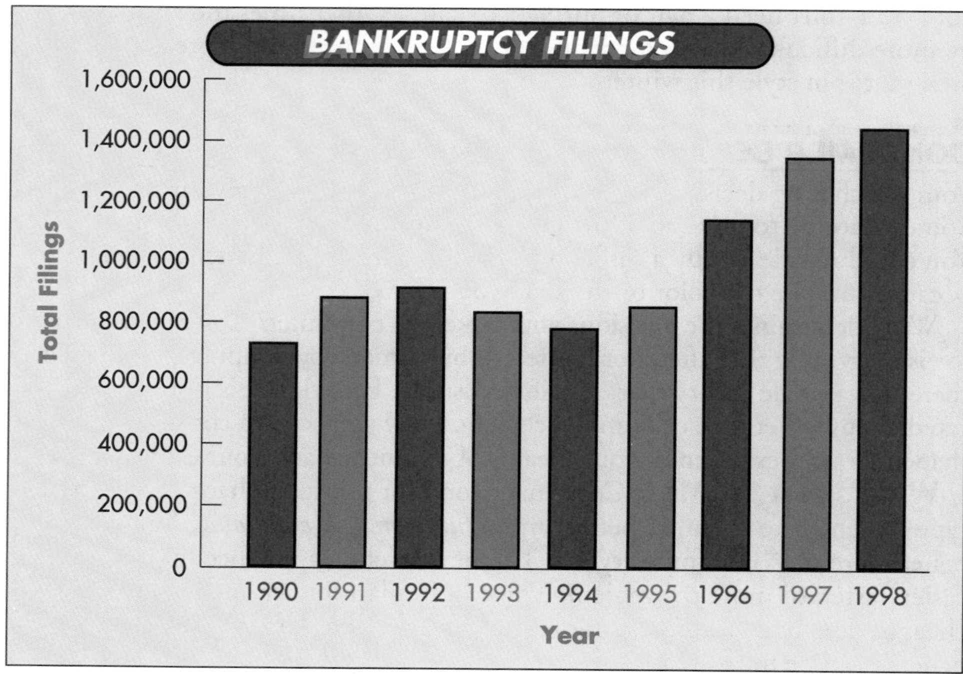

How do your needs and wants determine what you buy?

ADVERTISING IMPACT

After you have decided that there is something you need or want to buy, how do you choose which item meets your needs? This is when advertising becomes important.

An **advertisement** is a paid public announcement, usually emphasizing desirable qualities, to persuade you to buy an item or a service. Companies advertise to convince you, the consumer, to buy their products. They hope to influence your decision so you will choose their product at the store and they will make money.

TYPES OF ADVERTISING

There are several different types of advertisements, which are meant to influence you in different ways. Most ads combine information with entertainment, hoping to get and keep your attention long enough to hear the message and remember it when you go shopping.

Brand Advertising Brand advertising is intended to make you remember a brand rather than a specific product. This type of advertising is especially useful for companies that make several products, such as automotive parts, or a family of similar products, such as cookies.

Brand advertising has affected your buying decision if you have ever tried a new variety or flavor just because you have used or eaten an earlier product under the same brand label. A company that already sells several types of cookies is likely to successfully launch a new type of cookie. A new company would not have loyal customers ready to try its new cookies.

Informative Advertising Informative advertising teaches you about the product's benefits. This is useful for product benefits a consumer doesn't understand. Advertisements for medical products or services may need to inform potential customers of the condition the product treats before a company can sell it. Other products or product features, such as antilock brakes, become important selling features after customers are educated about the benefits.

List several television advertisements of each type. Select the one you think is most effective in each category. Why is it better than the others in the same category? Defend your decision to the class.

There were 1,408,041 bankruptcy filings in 1998. In 1990, that number was 718,107. Calculate the percent of increase in bankruptcy filings between 1990 and 1998.

SOLUTION

To determine the percent of increase, first subtract the number of 1990 filings from the number of 1999 filings. Then, divide the result by the number of 1990 filings.

$$\frac{\text{1999 Filings} - \text{1990 Filings}}{\text{1990 Filings}} =$$

$$\frac{1{,}408{,}041 - 718{,}107}{718{,}107} = 0.96\text{, or } 96\%$$

Bankruptcy filings increased by 96% from 1990 to 1998.

Informative ads can be helpful. For example, it was widely advertised in 1999 that taking aspirin could help during the early stage of a heart attack. However, the main purpose of the advertisement was to sell the product.

Select a product and a type of advertising. Draw an advertisement for the product that fits the advertising type.

Comparative Advertising Comparing the benefits or qualities of two or more similar products is comparative advertising. The advertised product will always win. After all, a company won't spend money on an ad to tell you its product is not as good as the one right next to it on the store shelf!

Comparative ads emphasize the strengths of the advertised product and the weaknesses of other products. If the qualities they emphasize are ones that are important to you, they will influence your decision. For example, extra legroom is important to a car shopper who is tall.

Defensive Advertising The losing product in a comparison ad may respond with a defensive advertisement. The company wants to tell consumers the weakness was exaggerated or that their product is better than the competitor in some other way.

Defensive ads are very similar to comparative ads. They are usually a response to the original comparison made by the competitor. Like the comparative ad, it can influence your decision if the features are product qualities important to you.

Persuasive Advertising These ads don't provide information, emphasize product features, or make comparisons. Instead they show happy people using the product. The implication is that you will be happier, more glamorous, more athletic, and so on. All you have to do is use the same product.

These advertisements influence your decisions because you want to be more like the person in the ad. Because these ads don't provide any useful information, they rely on emotional appeal. Don't let this type of advertising influence your decisions.

SUCCESSFUL ADVERTISING

Advertisers must try to understand your behavior as a consumer. Advertisements need to emphasize benefits that appeal to potential customers. For example, it wouldn't be smart for a company to advertise cars of a certain color rather than the design, style, or function of the car. Knowing what motivates your purchase helps car companies design advertisements that will influence your next purchasing decision.

Sometimes the success of a product can be traced directly to the product advertising. Some good products fail because of bad advertising. Other products succeed initially only because of good advertising. Ultimately a poor product will fail regardless of the quality of the advertising. A good commercial may get you to try a new restaurant. However, if the food and service are terrible, you probably won't go back. Repeat business and reputation also are important to success.

CHECKPOINT

What type of advertisement is a response to comparative advertising? What information does it provide?

____

____

THINK CRITICALLY

1. What is the difference between a need and a want?

2. What are the two types of benefits consumers want in the products they buy?

3. What is an example of consumer behavior?

4. Which type of advertising should you ignore? Explain.

5. Can a poor product succeed if it is well advertised?

MAKE CONNECTIONS

6. **COMMUNICATION** Amelia Sturling is sitting in her new art gallery waiting for customers to find her. Write her a one-page recommendation of things she could do to make customers come to her.

7. **RESEARCH** Using the library or Internet, determine the amount of money a large company spent on marketing or advertising. Prepare a presentation about your findings.

8. **GEOGRAPHY** Make a map of two grocery stores near your school or home. Mark the locations. How far apart are the two stores? Compare ads for the two stores. How do they compete against each other?

LESSON 1.2
THE CONSUMER IS IN CHARGE

DESCRIBE the relationship between your values and advertising

EXPLAIN the advantages and disadvantages of advertising

VALUES AND ADVERTISING

Spend an hour watching television, and you may see your own reflection. Commercials try to sell items that meet your needs, soothe your worries, and fill your dreams. The same messages bombard you from every direction. Look through a magazine, drive down a highway, or go to a sporting event, and you will see the same messages.

According to advertisements, Americans need cars, jewelry, and food. You worry about your weight, yellow teeth, and illness. You dream about owning expensive jewelry, driving luxury cars, and relaxing on sandy white beaches. Sometimes you have to wonder if you are reflected *by* the advertising or if you are a reflection *of* the advertising?

HOW DO YOU SEE YOURSELF?

The images you see in advertisements reflect two different visions of yourself—as you really are and as you wish you were. How do the images compare?

ON THE $CENE

Amelia Sturling finally realized she would have to do something to draw attention to her gallery/art supply store. The gallery is currently displaying art created by local artists. She thinks she should use the local focus of the show to attract interest from potential local customers. Amelia is looking for two kinds of customers, one to buy the artwork and one to buy the art supplies. For now, she wants to concentrate on the art supply side of her business. Amelia is creating some fliers she plans to distribute at an art school in the neighborhood. What are some ways she can appeal to potential customers?

How Do You Look? Advertisements will often show the consumer in the ad, hoping you can see yourself using the product. Yet individuals in the ads are usually portrayed as you wish you looked. The women are tall and slim, while the men are even taller with strong athletic builds.

These images aren't very accurate. The average female mannequin is 6 feet 2 inches tall, although the average woman is 5 feet 4 inches tall. Models in advertisements weigh 23 percent less than the average woman. The average man is 5 feet 9 inches tall. Disabled people are rarely seen in advertisements, even though 43 million Americans are disabled.

Where Do You Live? Most houses in advertisements are large, sunny, and spotless, even if the advertisement is for cleaning supplies. Neighborhoods have large lawns, shady trees, and friendly neighbors.

In 1997, the median size of a single-family, stand-alone house was 1,750 square feet. Of course, everyone doesn't live in a house. Many people live in apartments, mobile homes, duplexes, etc.

What Do You Think? Stereotypical images are still common in advertising. A stereotype is a standardized mental picture that some people think is true. The stereotype represents an oversimplified opinion or a prejudiced attitude or judgment. Critics believe that showing these stereotypes in advertising reinforces the attitudes in the audience.

The portrayal of women and minorities is often not in sync with today's world. Women in commercials are often portrayed as homemakers, despite the fact that many women are not only part of the workforce, they also hold many top management positions. Minorities are often portrayed as athletes rather than successful businesspeople.

WHY AREN'T THE IMAGES REALISTIC?

To some extent, these images are realistic. Remember that advertisements try to show their products in a positive way. Therefore, most images will also be positive. Large beautiful houses in the real world need to be cleaned, just like small cramped houses. Tall muscular men are just as likely to drink cola or eat out as anyone else.

Your Values The difference between how you are and how you are portrayed becomes a problem only if you forget that it is not usually the average person in the advertisements. Comparing yourself to the ideal that is often shown can create dissatisfaction or poor self-image in men and women alike.

Your values can affect the values shown in advertisements, but the advertisements also affect you. You must choose your own priorities and make your own decisions.

What two versions of yourself do you see in advertisements?

____

____

List several products you usually see advertised in your favorite magazine or during your favorite television show. Do these advertisements show average people? How realistic are the images they show?

PROS AND CONS OF ADVERTISING

Like anything else, there are good points and bad points, advantages and disadvantages, to advertising. Some impact you as an individual. Others impact your family, community, and society. **Society** is a community, group, or large grouping of people with common traditions, institutions, and activities and interests.

ADVERTISING PROVIDES INFORMATION

Each advertisement provides information for consumers. How this information is understood and used differs from person to person.

Advantage: Advertising Educates Consumers Advertising teaches you about the purpose, features, benefits, and value of the advertised product. Advertisements equip you with the information you need to make wise purchasing decisions. They also reduce **search time**, the amount of time you would spend to find products or services you want. Educated consumers improve their lives in several ways.

1. They buy better products.
2. They pay lower prices.
3. They spend less time shopping.

Disadvantage: Advertising Is Biased Advertising is not meant just to educate you. The purpose of an advertisement is to convince you to buy a product. It is biased, prejudiced, in favor of the product being advertised. Most advertisements contain little "pure" information about a product. Everything in the ad is there to make the product look good and convince you to buy it. An advertisement won't tell you the car feels small or didn't do well in a crash test.

COMPUTERS AND ADVERTISING The first television commercial with computer-generated footage was created in 1968. The *Star Wars* feature film was released in 1977, but computer-generated effects were not yet common for television. By 1979, computer-generated commercials were released, including Volkswagen, Chevrolet, and "Live From Lincoln Center." In 1991, PIXAR created ads for Listerine, Life Savers, and Tropicana that set a new standard for broadcast excellence. In 1993, computer graphics took a giant leap forward in the film *Jurassic Park.* Within a few years, the same technology was found in television commercials as well.

THINK CRITICALLY Why is the newest technology used for television commercials?

ADVERTISING RAISES THE STANDARD OF LIVING

The **standard of living** is the minimum level of necessities and luxuries required to maintain an individual or a group at a common level of comfort. It is usually based on income. The standard of living in an undeveloped country is much lower than it is in the United States.

The standard of living can vary within a single country, state, or community. In one part of town, it may be common for a family to own a single television, placed in the living room for shared viewing. In another part of town, a family might have a large television in a common area and smaller sets in the kitchen and every bedroom.

Advantage: Advertising Makes Products Cheaper Advertising helps a company sell more items. To keep up with the demand, a company has to make more of the items at the same time, which is cheaper for the company. If the company passes this on to you, each item will be cheaper.

If the company's profits increase, they can put more money into developing better products. The improved products also raise the standard of living. Advertising stimulates demand and keeps you informed about new products.

Disadvantage: Advertising Only Raises the Standard of Living for Some Advertising doesn't raise your income. If you can't afford a new car or dishwasher, advertising won't do anything for your standard of living. Advertising may widen the gap between the rich and the poor. The rich will be equipped with even more laborsaving devices or luxury items.

ADVERTISING AFFECTS YOUR HAPPINESS

Happiness is difficult to measure for an individual or a society. However, there is a relationship between the two.

Advantage: Advertising Reflects Society's Priorities Advertising promotes the good life. The good life is full of glamour, romance, and good friends. These pictures give you something to dream of and work toward.

Disadvantage: Advertising Promotes Materialism The good life promoted by advertising also contains material goods. Societies that have a high level of advertising can be materialistic. Advertisements promote products as symbols of status and success.

Individuals pursue personal satisfaction by purchasing material goods. This can hurt society in a variety of ways. For example, you might choose a high-income career rather than social work, teaching, or nursing. A school levy might not pass because local residents don't want to pay higher taxes. This hurts society as a whole.

Clio is the world's largest advertising awards competition. Starting in 1959, Clio recognizes advertising excellence worldwide in the areas of TV, Print, Outdoor, Radio, Integrated Media, Package Design, Student, and Web Sites.

ADVERTISING AFFECTS THE MASS MEDIA

Mass media is a form of communication designed to reach a large number of people. Magazines, newspapers, television, and radio are examples of mass media.

Advantage: Advertising Supports a Variety of Mass Media

Mass media is supported by advertising. In 1997, advertisers spent nearly $188 billion in the United States. Worldwide an estimated $450 billion was spent on advertising.

Money spent on advertising gives you low-cost access to a variety of information and entertainment providers. Television and radio broadcasts would not be free without support from advertisers. The price of magazines and newspapers would be much higher than their current cost. Specialized programs or magazines might not survive without advertising support.

Disadvantage: Advertising Affects the Information Available

Advertisers can shape the content of the media they support. In magazines or newspapers, advertisers can withdraw their ads if the publication prints something disagreeable to the advertiser. Publications with a small target audience or new publications could go out of business if a large advertiser withdraws support.

Advertisers buy airtime during popular television or radio programs. New programs come and go quickly if they can't draw an audience within a short time period. Quality programs that draw a smaller, more selective audience may be dropped in favor of mass-market programs. Shows that tackle controversial topics could also have trouble attracting advertisers.

How does advertising affect the mass media it supports?

____

____

THINK CRITICALLY

1. What stereotypes are often found in advertisements?

2. How do educated consumers improve their lives?

3. How does advertising raise the standard of living?

4. How could advertisers exert control on the mass media?

MAKE CONNECTIONS

5. **COMMUNICATION** After a favorite television show is canceled, two of your friends are debating the role of advertising in television programming. Choose a side, and explain several reasons why your position is correct.

6. **PROBLEM SOLVING** What suggestions would you make to Amelia Sturling about advertising her gallery or art supply business?

7. **SOCIAL STUDIES** Use the library or Internet to research the standard of living in another country. Compare the country to the United States. Write a short report about your findings.

LESSON 1.3

ADVERTISING AND THE ECONOMY

DESCRIBE the role of advertising in a company

DISCUSS the role of advertising in the economy

WHAT IS ADVERTISING?

Advertising is making paid public announcements to persuade consumers to buy an item or a service. To put it simply, to be an advertisement, three criteria must be met.

1. The message must be paid for.
2. The message must be delivered to the audience by mass media.
3. The message must try to persuade the audience of some action or belief.

Companies purchase advertisements because they hope to influence your consumer decisions. They want you to choose their product so they will make money.

ON THE $CENE

Amelia Sturling started taking action to draw attention to her gallery/art supply store. Because the gallery is currently displaying art created by local artists, she wants to use the local focus of the show to attract interest from potential local customers. To attract customers to buy art supplies, Amelia hung several posters and fliers at an art school in the neighborhood and purchased advertising space in their school paper. To attract customers to her gallery, she designed a listing for the next release of the local phone book. She also volunteered to be interviewed by the local newspaper. Why is this important to her business?

ADVERTISING IS A MARKETING TOOL

Advertising is part of a company's business process. It is a basic business tool that enables the company to communicate with customers. This is just as true for a small art gallery as it is for a multinational corporation.

Advertising is an important part of a company's marketing process. The process includes researching, pricing, promoting, selling, and distributing a product or service. Advertising relates to four marketing responsibilities.

1. Design a marketing strategy.
2. Make the product stand out, and target a market segment.
3. Contribute to revenue and profit earning.
4. Enhance customer satisfaction.

Marketing Strategy A marketing strategy is used to promote and distribute a product. The strategy includes advertisements you see and a long list of things you don't notice as much, such as warranties and instruction manuals.

Advertising tells the target audience about the value of the product or service. You must see the product's value before you will spend your money to buy it. Advertising messages must fit with the marketing strategy. For example, you don't want to advertise "easy to upgrade" if upgrades are expensive and difficult.

Stand Out in the Crowd Advertisers must make a product stand out from other products that are similar. You must think the product is different. If you think it is different, you will have a reason to choose one product or the other.

Imagine that two cans of chicken noodle soup are sitting on the store shelf. Brand A advertises that it has larger chunks of chicken. Brand B advertises that your mom gave you this soup to help you feel better when you were younger. If you only eat chicken noodle soup when you have a cold, which brand will you buy? If you really like chicken in your chicken noodle soup, which brand will you buy? Of course, Brand A never claimed to have more chicken, just larger chunks of chicken. You might think Brand A has more chicken.

Target the Consumer Targeting the type of consumer most likely to purchase the product is an important part of advertising. One of the key elements of many advertisements is including people that look like the target consumer. If you identify with the ad, you could see yourself buying and using the product or service.

This trend is easy to spot when you watch car commercials on television. Commercials for trucks and cars are obviously aimed at two different groups of consumers.

Choose a product that you have not discussed before. What sets it apart from similar items? Do you think it really is different from similar items, or is the difference only perceived?

Contribute to Revenue The purpose of the marketing process is the generation of revenue. Advertising also plays an important role in revenue generation by creating sales.

Brand Loyalty Advertising also inspires consumers to be loyal to a specific brand. This loyalty results from habit, brand images, and brand names. Consumers who are loyal to a brand are not sensitive to price increases. They will continue to buy the same brand, regardless of an increase in price.

Enhance Customer Satisfaction Advertisements that attracted consumers to buy a product will reinforce the decision after the item is bought and used. This reinforcement raises the customer's satisfaction level.

Life of the Product As you can see, good advertising generates revenue and profits throughout the lifetime of the product. It also enhances customer satisfaction before and after the sale.

How does advertising affect customer satisfaction?

___

___

ADVERTISING IN THE ECONOMY

Small businesses and multinational companies use advertising. Some aspects of advertising affect the economic system of the entire country and beyond.

GROSS DOMESTIC PRODUCT

The *gross domestic product* (GDP) is a measurement of the total value of all the goods and services produced within an economic system, usually that of an individual country. Within a company, advertising is part of the marketing strategy that produces sales. Advertising also contributes to consumer demand for products.

Advertising informs you about the features and benefits of each new product and tells you when the new products are available. As demand for a product grows, consumer spending increases in other categories. Thus, the GDP is affected by the sale of new products.

MARKET ECONOMY

An *economic system* is the way a nation uses resources to produce goods and services. The economic system in the United States, and most industrialized nations, is a *market economy*, which means that individuals, not the government, own the resources and run the businesses.

The purpose of most businesses in a market economy is to earn a profit. *Profit* is the difference between the cost of making and selling the product and the money you receive from selling it.

Supply and Demand Supply and demand rule a market economy. *Demand* is the quantity that consumers can buy at various prices during a given time period. Demand will go up if the price goes down.

Supply is the quantity that a supplier is willing to sell during a given time period. The supply will go up if the price goes up.

Basically, the buyer wants to buy at a low price. The seller wants to sell at a high price. The price where the buyer and the seller meet is the equilibrium price. How does advertising fit into the picture?

Advertising Affects the Demand Companies advertise because it increases their profit by increasing the demand. If customers want the product more, they will be willing to pay more. The equilibrium price will be higher. The company will make more money, and the consumers will still be satisfied even though they are paying a higher price.

BUSINESS CYCLES

Business operates in times of prosperity and recession. A recession is an economic downturn. To fight an economic downturn, some businesses increase spending on advertising, hoping to "buy" their way out of the downturn. Evidence does suggest that companies that maintain advertising during a recession perform better when the economy recovers compared to companies that cut advertising during a recession.

COMPETITION

Although the topic is still debated, it is commonly believed that advertising stimulates competition between companies. The competition motivates companies to develop new products and better methods of making the products. Advertising also can provide a way for companies to break into other markets, creating competition across the economy.

On the other side, it takes a large amount of money to advertise effectively. A company could be eliminated as a competitor because it lacks the money necessary to compete in the advertising arena.

ADVERTISING IN CHINA

Many experts believe that the Chinese economy will grow about 9 percent every year. In cities, retail sales rose 25 percent each year from 1995 to 1997. As the average Chinese income rises, China will continue to be an important consumer market.

China's advertising market has been marked as the eighth largest in the world. Advertising spending in 1996 was estimated at $3.9 billion. As new brands and products are introduced, retailers face competition in the market. The advertising market has room for growth, providing opportunity for American companies hoping to expand into the Chinese market. A 1996 survey showed that advertising in China averaged $3 per person. Advertising in America for the same time period averaged $330 per person.

THINK CRITICALLY What factors make the Chinese market attractive to U.S. retailers? What role will advertising play?

PRICES

Advertising affects price in both directions. The cost of advertising increases the cost of the product. This cost is passed on to the customer. On the other hand, advertising lowers the cost by increasing the demand. The company makes more of the items at the same time, lowering the production cost of each item.

How Much Do Companies Spend? Across all industries, advertising ranges from 1 percent of sales in the auto and retail industry to 15 percent in the personal care and luxury items business. Companies spend different amounts for advertising based on the industry, product, and market conditions. This makes it difficult to use a company's sales to predict how much it will spend on advertising.

VALUE

Branded products have symbolic value. The brand provides satisfaction that is worth more than the amount the customer pays to buy the branded product.

Social meaning is the interpretation of a product or service in a social context. The product's connection to a higher social class addresses a need to move up in social class. Products take meaning from culture and society. The meaning of a product can become a part of the product, just as its physical characteristics are part of the product.

How does advertising affect supply and demand?

THINK CRITICALLY

1. List the criteria a message must meet to be an advertisement.

2. Why do people in advertisements look like the target consumer?

3. How does advertising enhance customer satisfaction?

4. Why is a branded product more expensive?

MAKE CONNECTIONS

5. **COMMUNICATION** Suppose you are being interviewed for an entry-level position in the marketing department. The manager asks you to explain why advertising is important. Write a one-page description of your answer.

6. **PROBLEM SOLVING** AJ Sprockets needs to sell more widgets. What suggestions would you make to the marketing department?

7. **SOCIAL STUDIES** Use the library or Internet to research a different economic system. What role does advertising play in the system? Write a short report about your findings.

REVIEW

CHAPTER SUMMARY

LESSON 1.1 Needs and Wants

A. Your purchases are based on your needs and wants. A need is something you can't live without, and a want is something you can live without. It is very important to know the difference between a need and a want when evaluating advertising.

B. Each type of advertising is designed to influence your needs and wants in a different way.

LESSON 1.2 The Consumer Is in Charge

A. Advertising reflects your priorities and values. Sometimes advertising presents an idealized version of life, rather than a realistic one.

B. There are many advantages and disadvantages to advertising that impact you and your society. Among the advantages of advertising are that it provides product information and it makes products cheaper. Among the disadvantages of advertising are that ads can be more biased than informative and it can make products more expensive.

LESSON 1.3 Advertising and the Economy

A. Advertising is an important part of the marketing process. It is a message that must be paid for, must be delivered by mass media, and must try to persuade the audience to do or believe something.

B. Advertising affects the local, national, and global economies. Advertising can be used to help stimulate demand during economic downturns.

VOCABULARY BUILDER

Choose the term that best fits the definition. Write the letter of the answer in the space provided. Some terms may not be used.

____ **1.** The minimum level of necessities and luxuries required to maintain an individual or a group at a common level of comfort

____ **2.** Form of communication designed to reach a large number of people

____ **3.** A paid public announcement, usually emphasizing desirable qualities, to persuade you to buy an item or a service

____ **4.** Someone who uses goods

____ **5.** The amount of time you would spend to find products or services you want

____ **6.** Something that you would like to have but can live without

____ **7.** Interpretation of a product or service in a social context

____ **8.** Everything that affects or is affected by human consumption

____ **9.** Something that you can't live without

a. advertisement
b. consumer
c. consumer behavior
d. mass media
e. need
f. search time
g. social meaning
h. society
i. standard of living
j. want

REVIEW CONCEPTS

10. How much of their income do Americans spend?

11. What is the difference between a functional benefit and an emotional benefit?

12. Why do advertisements provide biased information?

13. Why are models used in advertisements?

14. How does advertising educate consumers?

15. How does advertising promote materialism?

16. What type of airtime do advertisers prefer to buy?

17. Why does an advertiser want consumers to be loyal to a brand?

18. How do companies decide the amount to spend on advertising?

19. Why do companies advertise?

APPLY WHAT YOU LEARNED

20. Which type of advertising appeals to you most? Why?

21. If everyone in your class saw the same advertisement, would reactions be the same? Why or why not?

22. What products are advertised in your favorite magazine or during your favorite TV show? What does this say about you?

23. Did the information about advertising in this chapter affect your opinion about advertising? Why or why not?

24. Did the information about advertising in this chapter affect your consumer behavior? Why or why not?

25. Give an example of how one company's decision to advertise can affect the local, national, and global economies.

MAKE CONNECTIONS

26. **GOVERNMENT** Political advertisements meet the three requirements to be classified as ads. Do you think these ads should be regulated in any way? Explain your answer.

27. **PROBLEM SOLVING** Have you ever compared two similar products at a store? What information can comparison shopping provide?

28. **RESEARCH** Compare advertisements on the Internet to other types of advertisements. What differences do you notice?

29. **SOCIAL STUDIES** Research the economic system in China. What was the previous system? What kinds of problems has China faced during the transition? Write a brief paper about your findings.

30. **COMMUNICATION** Research an area in the United States with a low standard of living. Write one page describing a typical day in this area.

CAREERS IN ADVERTISING

EMA

Eric Mower and Associates (EMA) was rated as one of the "Top 100 Agencies" in the nation in 1999 by *Adweek* magazine. EMA employs almost 200 full-time employees in its offices in New York state and Atlanta, Georgia. The firm provides advertising, public relations, sales promotion, media planning and execution, direct marketing, marketing research, and multimedia development. Their list of clients includes Arby's, Starbucks Coffee Company, and Welch's Foods, Inc. Perks for employees include profit sharing and a business casual dress code.

A Graphic Designer supports the internal creative department teams. This person must possess skill and knowledge in computer graphic technology, as well as hand skills to prepare mockups, paginate dummies, and develop presentation boards.

A college education is required. Proficiency in current Mac software is also necessary. The agency evaluates an applicant's computer skills and reviews the applicant's portfolio.

THINK CRITICALLY

1. What appeals to you about EMA and the position of Graphic Designer?
2. Describe typical professional activities of a Graphic Designer.

THE ADVERTISING INDUSTRY

LESSONS

The Chapter 2 video for this module introduces the concepts in this chapter.

PROJECT

Advertising For Tiny Tot Security

PROJECT OBJECTIVES

- Use the advertising process to begin to plan an advertising campaign
- Select the services you would need from a full-service advertising agency

GETTING STARTED

Read through the Project Process below. Make a list of any materials you will need. Decide how you will get the needed materials or information.

- Your client is Tiny Tot Security, which has recently started a service targeted at working parents with children. It negotiates with the care provider (daycare or private) to place a video camera where the child is located. The real-time video will be fed to an Internet site, where the parent can log in at any time.
- Bring in advertising for related fields such as daycare, security, or surveillance.
- Make a list of the advertising options in terms of media. How can you reach your target audience?

PROJECT PROCESS

Part 1 **LESSON 2.1** List the features of your client's service and the benefits you think should be emphasized in the advertising. Decide on the image of the service you want to convey.

Part 2 **LESSON 2.2** Using the advertising process, decide if you will use an external facilitator or not. Explain your reasons. Plan your marketing mix. How will you utilize each media you chose?

Part 3 **LESSON 2.3** Use the descriptions of the services offered by a full-service agency. Describe the roles of each individual in the agency's departments in the full-service agency in terms of this project. Create a flowchart describing how your advertisement will develop at each step.

Part 4 **LESSON 2.4** Discuss the ethical issues of the product. How will they affect your advertising?

CHAPTER REVIEW

Project Wrap-up Draw the advertisement, and present it to the class. Be prepared to discuss the reasoning behind your choices.

LESSON 2.1
EVOLUTION OF ADVERTISING

DESCRIBE the history of advertising

DISCUSS future developments in advertising

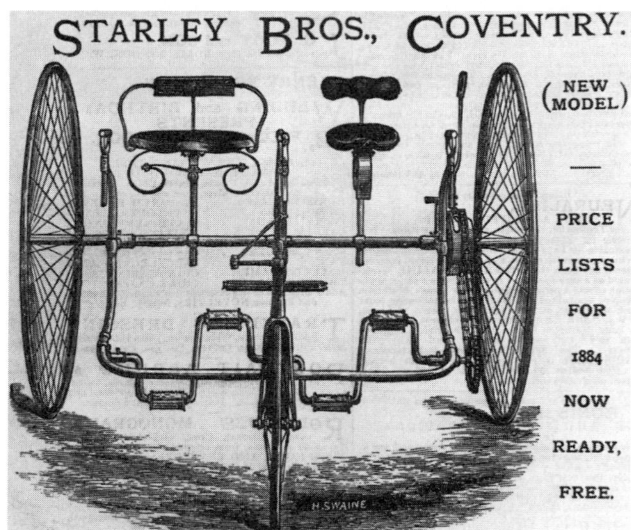

THE HISTORY OF ADVERTISING

Advertising is an important part of exchanging or purchasing goods. From the very first exchange, the seller has tried to convince potential buyers of the quality and benefits of the products for sale. Advertising, according to our requirements, is a recent development. Advertising is making paid public announcements using mass media to persuade consumers to buy an item or service. Therefore, even though early civilizations exchanged goods, it was not advertising because there was no mass media.

BEFORE ADVERTISING

Products and services were exchanged long before there was advertising. However, growing populations and population centers such as villages and towns set the stage for the birth and rise of advertising.

ON THE $CENE

Ray Dazai is the owner of five successful sandwich shops named Ray's Deli. The five shops are located in Indianapolis, Indiana. A competitor has recently gone out of business. She has offered to sell Ray her three shops in Indianapolis and two additional shops in Cincinnati, Ohio, less than two hours away. After agreeing to the purchase, Ray thinks it is time to create an advertising campaign. However, Ray doesn't know anything about advertising. What should he investigate?

Early Households Early households were *self-sufficient.* They were able to maintain themselves without outside assistance. For food, they grew crops and raised livestock. They designed and made clothing from cloth they created. They made yarn from wool and leather from cattle. They built houses from available materials such as stone and wood.

Early Towns As the population continued to grow, people gathered into towns for protection and commerce. Real estate was scarce in towns, and houses had little land around them. Residents were unable to remain self-sufficient. Without land, they could no longer grow food or raise livestock.

Residents began to specialize. Candlemakers made candles. Tailors made clothes. Specialized shops provided food such as fruit, bread, and meat. Residents became *interdependent.* They had to rely on others to make things they couldn't provide for themselves.

Early Commerce As individuals began to specialize, they also began to barter. They exchanged one commodity for another. The candlemaker traded candles to the baker in exchange for bread. The baker traded bread to the tailor in exchange for clothing.

As more people specialized, the barter system became outdated. It became too complicated to barter for everything. For example, the baker might want glass for his windows, but the glassmaker didn't want bread. People began to sell their products for something that everyone agreed was valuable — gold. A free market economy ruled by supply and demand was on the rise.

The American Advertising Museum is located in Portland, Oregon. It has a large collection of advertising artifacts. The museum is dedicated to preserving and interpreting American advertising. The museum also maintains a web site at www.admuseum.org.

ADVERTISING—IN THE BEGINNING

A free market economy is an important factor in the growth of advertising. Supply and demand inspires competing businesses to advertise to increase the demand for their products.

Before 1800 Towns became cities, creating large groups of people that could be targeted by advertising. New technology and inventions made it possible to distribute information to many people at the same time. Advertising was born.

In 1704, the *Boston News Letter* contained paid advertisements for items such as real estate and rewards for the return of stolen merchandise. These early advertisements were text only. Illustrations were not used in advertising until much later.

Industrial Revolution The Industrial Revolution changed the world in many ways. It began around 1750 in England and spread slowly until the 1800s. In 1850, the idea of making interchangeable parts and the introduction of the perfected sewing machine made mass production a possibility. If a company could make a large number of items, it needed to stimulate the demand for those items by advertising. For example, if Able Furniture could make 1,000 chairs, they needed to have customers who would buy 1,000 chairs. Advertising became necessary for growing businesses.

The 1800s Several other events in the 1800s produced a boom in business and advertising. The invention of the telegraph in 1844 created a means of communicating at great speed over long distances. Transportation was changed forever when the United States was connected from coast to coast by the railroad in 1864. It opened distant markets for local companies.

By 1850, newspaper circulation was estimated to reach one million copies per day. The mass media was ready to deliver advertising to over a million people a day. The first advertising agent, Volney Palmer, opened his doors for business in Philadelphia.

ADVERTISING MATURES

Advertising took a more modern look. Illustrations began to give advertisement the look you are accustomed to seeing today.

The 1900s Advertisements became more visual. In fact, some advertisements from the 1920s were so beautifully illustrated that they are considered to be works of art today. In the 1930s, the radio emerged as an effective advertising medium. Radio remained the most significant advertising medium until television appeared in the 1950s. By 1960, 90 percent of American homes had televisions.

Advertising thrived in the television arena. Initially, advertisements focused only on the product. Early television commercials were very different from the commercials of today. However, advertisers learned quickly. By the 1990s, commercials were slick and polished.

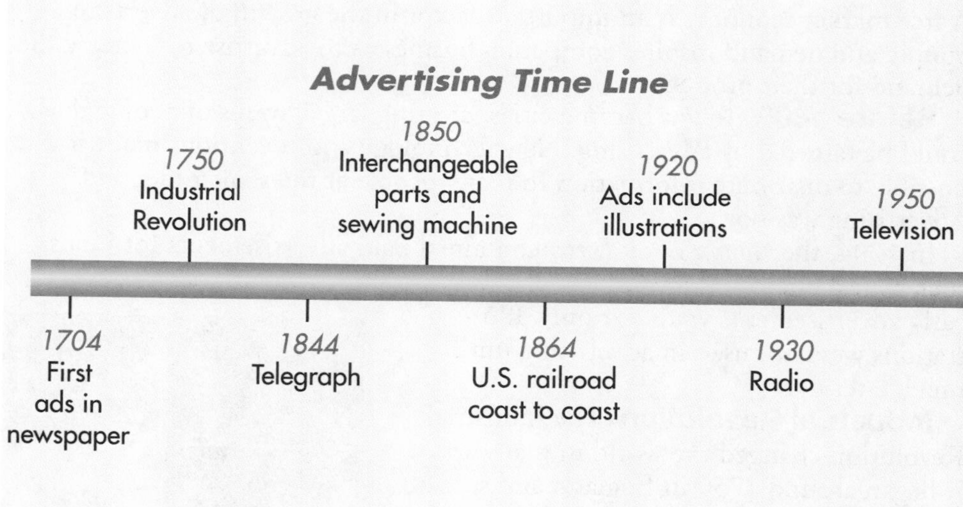

What impact did the Industrial Revolution have on advertising?

____

____

ADVERTISING—TODAY AND TOMORROW

Advertisers have learned from experience. Today's advertising is fast and slick. The consumer has learned, too. Today's audience is knowledgeable and sophisticated.

ADVERTISING—TODAY

Today advertising is everywhere. It's in the magazines and newspapers you read, on the radio you listen to, on the television you watch, at the sporting events you attend, on the signs you see, and the Internet you surf. It's impossible to avoid.

Depending on size and industry, companies can spend a large percentage of their income on advertising. This can amount to millions or billions of dollars. For example, Procter & Gamble, whose products include Tide laundry detergent and Crest toothpaste, spends $3 billion a year on advertising.

Advertising Media The traditional forms of media used to deliver advertising have matured. Traditional advertising media are directed at a passive audience. You read, listen, or watch passively.

Within the existing media, it is rare to produce an advertisement that is truly new or innovative. The various media have reached their limitations. Print ads are limited by what can be placed on paper. Radio ads are limited to sounds they can produce, and television ads are limited to sights and sounds. Advertising may yet overcome these limitations in the future.

The Internet Today Buying and selling on the Internet is clearly established and growing rapidly. Most large companies are already devoting part of their advertising budgets for Internet advertising. Although the role of advertising on the Internet is still developing, it seems to be working. In 1998, Internet advertising revenue was $1.92 billion. In 1999, that figure more than doubled, reaching $4.62 billion.

Remember that advertising supports most forms of mass media. However, the Internet performs so many functions that it is difficult to classify it as a form of mass media. Retailers were not the first kids on the block. The Internet was originally created to exchange information between scientists and researchers. Today it is a tool that informs, educates, entertains, communicates, and advertises.

ADVERTISING—TOMORROW

The future is difficult to predict. Surely, families gathered around the radio in the 1930s never would have anticipated families gathered around a television only a few decades later.

The Purpose of Advertising Regardless of predictions, it is important to remember one thing about advertising in the future. The definition of advertising won't change. It must still be a paid attempt to convince or

List the products you saw advertised today and the locations where they were advertised. Include items advertised on television, radio, newspapers, magazines, and billboards. Which advertisements were memorable and which barely registered with you?

persuade that is delivered through mass media. Its role in business won't change. It will continue to be a marketing tool that contributes to a company's revenue and profits by stimulating the demand for the company's products or services. Most changes in advertising will occur in the methods used to prepare the advertisements and the media used to deliver the message.

The Internet Tomorrow The spectacular growth of advertising revenue in the late 1990s proves that the Internet will continue to become an important part in advertising strategies of large and small companies. The Internet provides a level playing field for all companies. A small home-based business is almost as likely as a large multinational corporation to have a web site. Web sites serve as store windows, allowing customers to look in at the products. Advertising is necessary to attract attention to the web site.

Methods for delivering advertising will change as the Internet grows and evolves. Just as the original developers of the Internet did not envision the Internet of today, it is difficult to picture the Internet of tomorrow. Commerce and advertising will certainly be a part of the future Internet.

Interactive Media The main difference between the Internet and traditional advertising media is the potential for exchange between the consumer and the advertiser. The connection is *interactive.* This means that communication goes both ways. The consumer can provide input. Advertising doesn't have to be a passive experience for the consumer. This provides opportunities for advertisers. Internet advertising today doesn't take full advantage of this feature. Perhaps it will in the future.

Other forms of interactive media are currently in development. Major retailers have already tested interactive home shopping. Multimedia services from America Online and others may be delivered via cable. WebTV brings the Internet to you through your television. Many programs now tell you where to look on the Web for additional information. With WebTV, you can click on the interactive links displayed on the television screen while you watch the show. This is an enormous step forward for advertisers. It may be the foundation for even more advances in the future.

Future Technologies It may be possible in the future for advertisers to target and reach every consumer that might purchase their products. Something completely new may be on the drawing board right now that will change advertising in ways you can't begin to imagine. The potential for future technology is unlimited.

CHECKPOINT

What limitations exist for traditional advertising media?

____

____

____

THINK CRITICALLY

1. Describe the earliest advertisements.

2. Why was the development of towns and cities important to advertising?

3. How did the Industrial Revolution affect advertising?

4. Does advertising support the Internet? Explain.

5. What is the difference between traditional advertising and the Internet?

MAKE CONNECTIONS

6. **COMMUNICATION** Look at several advertisements on the Internet. How do these advertisements differ from ads in other media? Write a one-page summary of the differences you identify.
7. **HISTORY** Using the library or Internet, look up the Industrial Revolution. What impact did it have on the average person? Prepare an oral report about your findings.
8. **PROBLEM SOLVING** What advertising media would you recommend for a small business in your town? Explain your recommendation.

LESSON 2.2
ADVERTISING INDUSTRY

DESCRIBE the structure of the advertising industry

EXPLAIN the forces that may change the advertising industry

THE STRUCTURE OF THE INDUSTRY

An **industry** is a distinct group of productive or profit-making businesses. Some industries are easy to describe. The automobile industry makes cars. The steel industry makes steel. The fast food industry makes fast food. Is it accurate to say that the advertising industry makes advertisements? The answer is yes and no.

A business does hire an advertising agency to make advertisements for its products or services. That's not all it is buying though. It buys an idea, the way that the idea is expressed (the advertisement), a public image, a reputation, and, hopefully, an increase in customer traffic and revenue.

ON THE $CENE

After a recent expansion that doubled the number of sandwich shops from five to ten, Ray Dazai has been investigating the process of advertising. In the past, he has simply placed a few advertisements in local Indianapolis newspapers and distributed fliers and coupons to businesses and schools near his shops. Because two of the new shops are located in Cincinnati, Ohio, he doesn't think this approach will be as effective. Also, he is not familiar with the media or the competition in Cincinnati. Ray thinks it might be time to get advice from an advertising agency, but he isn't sure what an agency would do for his business. What arguments would you use to persuade him? Is there anything about his situation that would be an advertising challenge?

WHO BUYS ADVERTISING?

Remember that the purpose of advertising is to stimulate demand for a product or service, resulting in increased revenue and profit. With this in mind, every business could benefit from advertising.

How Much Do They Spend? The amount businesses spend annually varies, depending on the company's size, revenue, and industry. In the United States, companies currently spend about $200 billion on advertising every year. Globally, advertisers spend $425 billion. Those figures grow about 7 to 8 percent a year.

In 1997, the top 100 advertisers in the United States spent a total of $58 billion dollars on advertising. That same year, General Motors alone spent $3 billion on advertising. That seems like a lot to spend until you realize that $3 billion is only 3 percent of GM's sales.

THE ADVERTISING PROCESS

The advertising industry is composed of individuals with talent and specialized expertise. These individuals perform specific functions in planning, creating, and distributing advertisements.

The Process A business starts the process by deciding to advertise. It can either hire an advertising agency or design its own advertising. The agency or the advertising department designs the advertisements. It can do everything or choose to use an external facilitator to perform tasks such as advertising research and physical production of the advertising components. After the advertisement is produced, it must be placed in the media. All of this activity is aimed at you, the consumer.

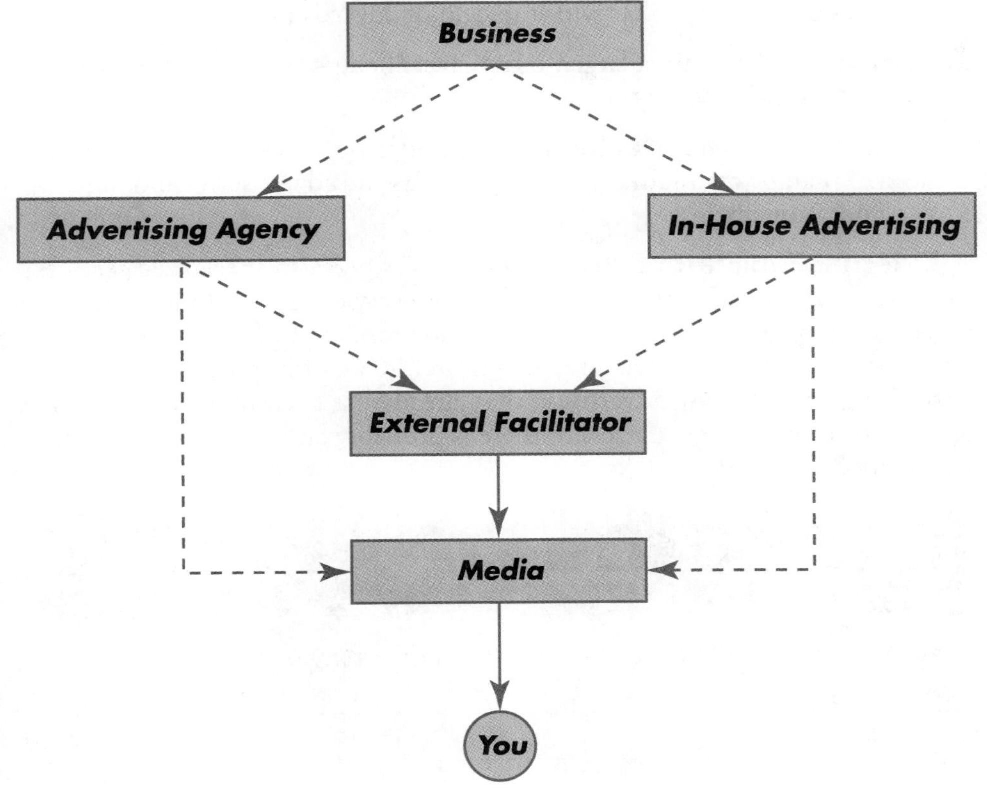

Advertisers Businesses use advertising in different ways. Manufacturers of consumer goods and services advertise the most. Procter & Gamble and General Foods provide products such as laundry detergent and food. Service providers include hospitals, beauty shops, restaurants, and organizations such as your local symphony and museum.

Retailers buy products to sell to consumers. Retailers include stores such as grocery stores, clothing stores, and department stores. All of these rely on newspapers, television, radio, and billboards to advertise their business. Wholesalers buy products to sell to manufacturers or retailers. Because their target audience is much smaller, they rely on trade publications, direct mail, and trade shows for advertising.

The U.S. government is also an advertiser. It spent more than $620 million in 1997. When the U.S. Mint made the first gold $1 coin, it launched an extensive ad campaign that included national broadcast, print, radio, transit, and Internet advertising and featured George Washington as spokesman for the Golden Dollar. The government also advertises heavily for military recruits.

Choose a local retail store you have seen or heard advertised. List all the locations you have noticed advertising for the store. Was the store advertised on radio or television? Have you seen billboards or signs? Is there a single message carried through all the advertising media?

Advertising Agency An **advertising agency** is a company made up of professionals who specialize in providing creative and business services involved in planning, preparing, and placing advertisements. Agencies can provide many different services, from creating advertisements to measuring the effectiveness of the advertising. Some specialize in a specific part of the advertising process, such as buying media time or creating interactive media like CDs or Internet sites.

Because the main business of an advertiser is *not* advertising, most companies hire an advertising agency. This has several advantages over maintaining an in-house advertising department.

1. Businesses are not familiar with the field of advertising.
2. Agencies can maintain a larger, more diversified pool of specialists than an advertiser would employ.
3. It is more cost-effective to pay a consultant to do a specific task when it's needed than to maintain a staff of specialists the advertiser would only need occasionally.

External Facilitators External facilitators perform specialized services for advertisers and advertising agencies. These services can include a variety of tasks, such as providing sets, equipment, and work crews for commercials or photography sessions. Others provide research to assist in planning future advertising or evaluating advertising that already has been released. Regardless of the type of extra service needed, there is probably an external facilitator who can fill the need.

Do advertisers have to use external facilitators? Why or why not?

____

____

CHANGES IN THE ADVERTISING INDUSTRY

As the business world changes, the advertising industry must also change. Advertising has always been thought of as a leading-edge field—an industry that leads in creativity, innovation, and technology. To keep that reputation, the industry adapts to a world that changes daily.

NEW RETAIL CHANNELS

Today's consumers don't shop only in stores made of brick and mortar. Many prefer to shop from the comfort of their own homes. Catalogs, TV shopping networks, and online shopping are all relatively new shopping methods. For retailers, removing the need for a physical store and sales personnel seriously reduces costs. It also provides a sales outlet for small specialty retailers that can't afford the cost of a retail store.

These new retail channels bring new challenges for the advertising industry. The industry is currently wrestling with the question of how to reach consumers who would rather buy without leaving their homes.

MARKET SATURATION

As a consumer, you see advertisements everywhere you look. Even while you are buying one product, you are exposed to advertising for other products. Buy a ticket to a movie at the theater. Before the movie starts, you watch trailers for other movies scheduled to be released soon. During prime-time television programming, you watch almost 17 minutes of commercials. Daytime viewing is even more cluttered. You watch almost 21 minutes of commercials every hour during the day.

Advertising is becoming its own worst enemy. In this environment, it is a challenge to create an advertisement that will stand out and remain with the consumer.

ADVERTISING GLOBALLY

Many large advertising companies not only work for multinational corporations, they *are* multinational corporations. Agencies maintain offices in additional countries to provide a "home-court" advantage in obtaining various services and media placements in those countries. This practice also provides social and economic understanding of the country's culture. This ensures that the advertising message delivered is the intended message.

THINK CRITICALLY What advantages does a multinational advertising agency provide for a global advertising campaign?

INTEGRATED MARKETING COMMUNICATION

Frequently, businesses want to use an integrated approach to marketing communication. An advertisement does not stand alone. Instead it is part of the **marketing mix**. The marketing mix includes all marketing activities, such as advertising, sales promotions, event sponsorships, and public relations. The challenge is to stay within the borders of the company's marketing mix while creating an advertisement that is unique. The advertisement must integrate smoothly into the other activities in the marketing mix. A consistent message must be delivered through all of the marketing materials and events.

MEDIA CONSOLIDATION

Many media companies have merged in recent years. For example, in some cities, a single company can own several individual radio stations. This means that a single company can control more than 50 percent of the market in the city. This affects an advertiser's ability to negotiate costs for advertising. If an advertiser wants to buy advertising time on any of the radio stations, it must negotiate with the same company.

BUSINESS CONSOLIDATION

Media companies are not the only businesses that are consolidating. Companies in many industries are merging and consolidating. This affects the advertising industry in two ways.

1. Fewer businesses are potential clients.
2. Consolidated companies want to advertise in larger geographic areas.

FACING THE CHALLENGES

Some agencies have already begun to change to react to these challenges. Some full-service advertising agencies have reorganized to be able to devote a group of professionals to the new interactive retail channels such as the Internet. Many agencies have groups that specialize in creating web sites. In 1999, it was estimated that 78 percent of American advertising agencies had created web sites for a client, even though some of those agencies did not have web sites for themselves.

The consolidation of media companies is a source of major concern for advertising agencies. The cost of most forms of advertising has increased in recent years. At least part of this increase is a direct result of merging media companies. Advertisers will have to work together to change this situation.

What impact does the current amount of advertising have on the advertising industry?

____

____

THINK CRITICALLY

1. What does a business expect to get when it hires an advertising agency?

2. Name several new retail channels.

3. What does the marketing mix include?

4. How does media consolidation impact advertising?

MAKE CONNECTIONS

5. **COMMUNICATION** Suppose you are the director of marketing for a major fast food chain. What changes in the advertising industry concern you the most? Describe ways that your company might overcome these challenges.

6. **PROBLEM SOLVING** Suppose you work for an advertising agency. You need to purchase media time for radio and television commercials in a midsize city. Company A owns two radio stations, a television station, and a newspaper. Company B owns three radio stations that control the majority of the market share. Company C owns a small radio station, and Company D owns a midsize radio station. Describe your negotiation strategy.

7. **SOCIAL STUDIES** Suppose your company sells high-fashion clothing in the United States. In the spring, your company will merge with a smaller company that sells high-fashion clothing in Spain. How will this impact your marketing mix? Describe topics that you may need to research.

8. **GOVERNMENT** Suppose you are the president of an advertising agency. Your firm recently tried to negotiate to lower the cost of media time. However, a single company controlled 60 percent of the market share in the city. Write a letter to your congressperson or senator requesting stricter regulations for media businesses.

LESSON 2.3
ADVERTISING AGENCIES

DIFFERENTIATE between the services provided by different types of advertising agencies

DESCRIBE the organization and roles within the advertising agency

DIFFERENCES BETWEEN AGENCIES

All advertising agencies are not the same. They don't perform the same tasks for the client or operate in the same way. Some specialize in specific steps of the advertising process, specific business industries, or specific types of advertising. Generally there are five types of advertising agencies.

1. In-house agency
2. Full-service agency
3. Creative boutique
4. Media-buying services
5. Interactive agency

ON THE $CENE

Ray Dazai finally decided to hire an advertising agency. He has a few things to consider before he chooses an agency. His sandwich shops, which operate under the name Ray's Deli, are located in Indiana and Ohio. Currently, he doesn't do any real advertising besides a few local newspaper advertisements and fliers and coupons. His usual customers are students and businesspeople on lunch breaks. His business traffic drops dramatically evenings and weekends. The store locations he recently purchased were not successful for his competition. He wants to have radio and television commercials in both cities. Which of these facts helps you select the type of agency he should contact? Which type of agency would you recommend?

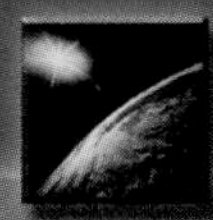

IN-HOUSE AGENCY

An **in-house agency** is an advertising department in a company whose main business is not advertising. Because the department is actually part of the business, it has several advantages and disadvantages.

Advantages	Disadvantages
Familiar with the company's products, industry, and business practices	Lack of objectivity
Better control and coordination of the advertising process	Won't try to improve the advertising by arguing for better options
Doesn't have to pay an advertising agency for its services	Lacks the depth and variety of experience that an agency can maintain

FULL-SERVICE AGENCIES

Full-service agencies provide a wide range of services designed to meet a client's complete advertising needs. In a typical full-service agency, client services include account management, marketing planning and management, creative design, production, media-planning, and media-buying services.

CREATIVE BOUTIQUE

A **creative boutique** specializes in developing creative concepts, writing creative text, and providing artistic services. This type of agency is usually hired by another agency to add greater creativity to the advertising message or add excitement to a single advertisement. The group that hired the creative boutique performs the other tasks of preparing and placing the advertisements or distributes the tasks to other specialized agencies.

MEDIA-BUYING SERVICES

A **media-buying service** specializes in buying media time and space, particularly on radio and television. Because the media-buying service buys large quantities of time, it can buy time at a lower cost. It resells the time to advertising agencies. This is a specialized service purchased by other agencies.

INTERACTIVE AGENCIES

Interactive agencies specialize in helping clients prepare advertising for new interactive media, such as the Internet, CD-ROMs, and interactive television. These services require specific expertise that isn't common yet in many full-service agencies. Interactive agencies can maintain Internet sites and build databases. This special service is often purchased by other agencies.

Why would an in-house agency hire a specialized service provider?

____

____

THE ROLES OF INDIVIDUALS IN THE INDUSTRY

If you are a member of the advertising industry, your role is tied to the function of your department or agency. Like any other industry, you would start at an entry-level position and work your way up to a position with more responsibility or management tasks as you gain experience.

Every agency will not follow this exact structure, but this gives you a good idea of the roles individuals play in the daily tasks. A typical full-service advertising agency can divide its services into six categories—account services, marketing services, creative services, production services, media services, and administrative services.

ACCOUNT SERVICES

Account services include identifying the benefits of the client's product, the possible consumers to target with advertising, and the best positioning against competing products. With this information, an agency develops a complete advertising plan. Services sometimes include research.

Account services managers are often known as account executives, account supervisors, or account managers. Their primary duty is keeping the agency teams working on the account on schedule and within budget. They also work with the client and creative services to create effective advertisements using the correct cultural and consumer values. *Analysts* research to identify the consumer's behavior and values.

MARKETING SERVICES

Marketing services include research, sales promotion and event sponsorship, direct marketing, and public relations. The agency will locate previous studies related to the product's market or objectives. The agency might recommend events to be sponsored, such as races or golf tournaments.

Event-marketing specialists identify if and how the business should support different events. *Researchers* study areas such as advertising results and target audiences.

CREATIVE SERVICES

Creative services develop the advertising message. They use words and images to deliver that message to consumers.

The creative group usually includes a creative director, art director, illustrator, and copywriters. The *creative director* manages the group and ensures that the art and text come together to create the desired results on schedule. The *art director* manages the art production for the group, ensuring the quality of the graphics for each project. The *illustrator* draws or creates the graphics for each project.

Select one of the job titles in the advertising industry that most interests you. Write a paragraph describing why it interests you, what skills you have now that you think fit the position, and how you can learn other skills you might need for the position.

Advertising agencies are often paid a commission. A commission is usually a percentage based on sales made or money earned. However, for an advertising agency, the commission is based on how much the advertiser spends on media. If Widget Works spends $1 million on television airtime and its commission rate is 15 percent, how much will it pay Able Agency to create the advertising?

SOLUTION

Commission = Amount spent on media × Commission rate
Commission = $1,000,000 × 0.15
Commission = $150,000

The agency earns $150,000 for creating the advertising.

Today graphics are frequently created with specialized software. An illustrator "draws" with a computer as well as a pencil. *Copywriters* write the text, also called copy, that works with the images. Well-written advertising copy creates images and emotions that persuade the audience to purchase the product.

PRODUCTION SERVICES

Production services produce polished advertising messages. The production crew brings the images and words to life for radio and television commercials. The crew includes *producers* and their *assistants.* Print and television advertisements require producers to create the desired effect.

MEDIA SERVICES

A large portion of the client's money is spent on buying media time or space. Media services also determine the consumers who will be reached by the message. These two factors make media services very important. *Media planners, media buyers,* and *media researchers* help the client choose the most effective media options within the client's budget. The array of new interactive media options makes guidance important for undecided clients.

ADMINISTRATIVE SERVICES

Advertising agencies are just like any other business in some ways. They have accounting, personnel, and billing departments, as well as a sales department that sells the agency's services to clients. *Traffic management* falls under administrative services. *Traffic managers* ensure that creative services and media services coordinate so that ads are ready for the media placement deadline.

What is the primary duty of account services managers?

____

____

How does a creative boutique fit into a full-service agency's needs? List reasons why a full-service agency might hire a creative boutique.

THINK CRITICALLY

1. What are the advantages of working with an in-house agency?

2. Why are interactive agencies often hired by full-service agencies?

3. What are the six types of services a full-service agency provides?

4. Why are media services one of the most important services offered?

MAKE CONNECTIONS

5. **RESEARCH** Use the library or Internet. Select one of the roles in an advertising career that interests you. Write a summary of the education and experience needed for the job.

6. **COMMUNICATION** Suppose you are applying for your dream job at Able Agency several years from now. Describe the experience you will have listed on your resume. What position would you apply for, and how will this experience qualify you for the position?

7. **PROBLEM SOLVING** A potential client is debating between hiring your creative boutique, then creating the advertising with an in-house agency, and hiring a full-service agency. How would you convince him to hire your agency?

8. **ECONOMICS** Some advertisers and agencies don't think it is fair to base the agency's commission on the amount spent on media. Why do they believe this? Describe a better method of compensating an agency for its work.

LESSON 2.4
REGULATIONS AND ETHICS

DESCRIBE how the advertising industry is regulated

DISCUSS the ethics of advertising

ADVERTISING REGULATIONS

Advertising is meant to persuade an audience to buy a certain product or believe a certain thing. If the purpose of advertising is to persuade, it makes sense that government agencies and laws should regulate advertising to protect consumers.

GOVERNMENT AGENCIES

Several government agencies regulate advertising in some way. Most of these agencies were established for some other reason. For example, the Library of Congress was established to protect copyrights. However, the Library of Congress would also be called on if it was thought that an advertisement infringed on an existing copyrighted communication.

ON THE $CENE

Ray Dazai is looking forward to working with an advertising agency. He has a few ideas about the advertising for his sandwich shops, Ray's Deli. He wants the advertising to appeal to his usual customers, students and businesspeople on lunch breaks. Two of his shops frequently attract a large number of high school students after school events. Although he wants to appeal to high school students, he wonders if there are laws that determine appropriate advertising for a target audience less than 18 years of age. Do you think advertising aimed at teenagers should be regulated?

Six government agencies have more impact on advertising regulations than other government agencies.

1. Federal Trade Commission (FTC)
2. Federal Communications Commission (FCC)
3. Food and Drug Administration (FDA)
4. Securities and Exchange Commission (SEC)
5. U.S. Postal Service
6. Bureau of Alcohol, Tobacco, and Firearms

Federal Trade Commission This agency, also known as the FTC, was created in 1914 to enforce laws prohibiting unfair methods of competition. In 1916, the FTC determined that false advertising was an unfair method of competition. This established advertising as a primary interest of the agency. Initially, the FTC dealt only with advertising that had a direct effect on the advertiser's competition. The Wheeler-Lea Amendment in 1938 expanded the FTC's authority to include advertising that was misleading to the public. The FTC could now force an advertiser to withdraw deceptive advertisements.

Throughout its existence, the FTC has continued to gain more authority over advertising regulations in the United States. The Wool Products Labeling Act in 1939, the Fur Products Labeling Act in 1951, and the Textile Fiber Products Identification Act in 1958 provided regulatory power over labeling and advertising for some products. The FTC's ability to protect consumers was enhanced by the Fair Packaging and Labeling Act in 1966, the Truth in Lending Act in 1969, and the Fair Credit Reporting Act in 1970.

More recently, the 1990 Nutrition Labeling and Education Act has expanded the agency's role in regulating labeling and advertising. The world of online and interactive advertising provides new challenges for the FTC.

Federal Communications Commission This agency, also known as the FCC, enforces laws prohibiting obscenity, fraud, and lotteries on radio and television stations. It is able to revoke a station's broadcast license if a station is in violation of the laws.

FTC INVESTIGATES CONSUMER PRIVACY ON THE INTERNET When you respond to advertising online, you provide personal information to the web site. The Federal Trade Commission is interested in protecting your personal information on the Internet. In May 2000, the FTC's Advisory Committee on Online Access and Security (ACOAS) submitted a report to the FTC about access and security of personal information collected by American web sites. The FTC is concerned about the information that is collected, the security protecting the information after it is collected, and the way the information is used.

THINK CRITICALLY What information would help a web site serve you better? Are you concerned that a web site has your personal information? How would you feel if the web site sold that information to other businesses?

Food and Drug Administration This agency, also known as the FDA, regulates, among other things, the advertising for food, drugs, cosmetics, and medical products. It can require special labeling for products considered to be dangerous, such as household cleaners. It also regulates labeling and packaging. It prosecutes false labeling.

Securities and Exchange Commission This commission enforces laws for the advertising of securities. It also regulates the disclosure of company information on the annual report.

U.S. Postal Service The Postal Service enforces laws for direct mail advertising. It prosecutes lotteries, fraud, and misrepresentation.

Bureau of Alcohol, Tobacco, and Firearms This agency, also known as the ATF, influenced advertising for alcoholic beverages by requiring warning labels on advertisements for alcoholic beverages and banning active athletes from appearing in commercials.

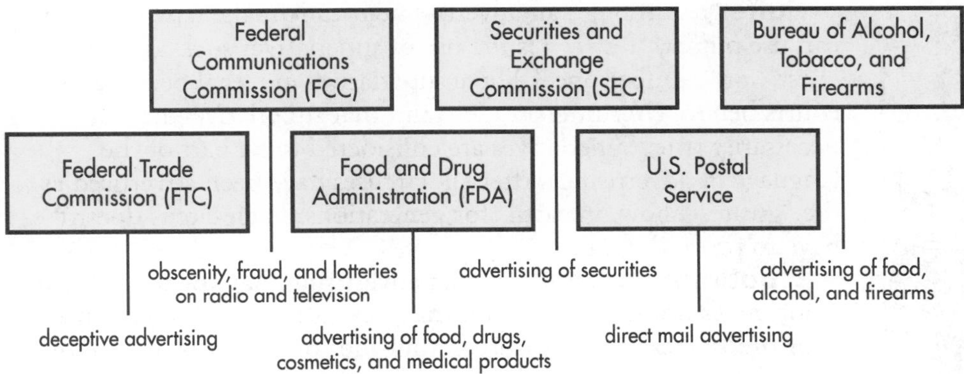

ADDITIONAL REGULATIONS

From time to time, additional regulations are passed on various topics related to advertising. For example, the Children's Television Act was passed in 1990. It limits the amount of commercial airtime to 10.5 minutes per hour on weekdays and 12 minutes on weekends during children's programming.

SELF-REGULATION

Self-regulation is an industry's attempt to regulate itself. The most important organization devoted to self-regulation is the Council of Better Business Bureau's National Advertising Review Board (NARB). NARB is part of the National Advertising Division (NAD) of the Council of Better Business Bureau. Complaints about advertising received by the Better Business Bureau are reviewed by NAD. If NAD can't resolve the complaint, the complaint is appealed to NARB, where a panel of advertisers evaluates the complaint. If the issue still can't be resolved, it is forwarded to the FTC or another regulatory agency.

Why was the Federal Trade Commission established?

ETHICS IN ADVERTISING

Ethics is a code of conduct based on what is good or bad and moral duty or obligation. Ethical behavior includes honesty, integrity, and fair play.

The purpose of a business is to make money. The purpose of advertising is to help the business make more money. Where does ethics fit into the picture?

COMPETITION AND DECEPTION

In sports, it's not considered fair to hurt someone on the other team to win the game. A team should win because it has better skills, not because it cheated.

Advertisers compete for your business. Like competition in any sports arena, competition between businesses should be fair.

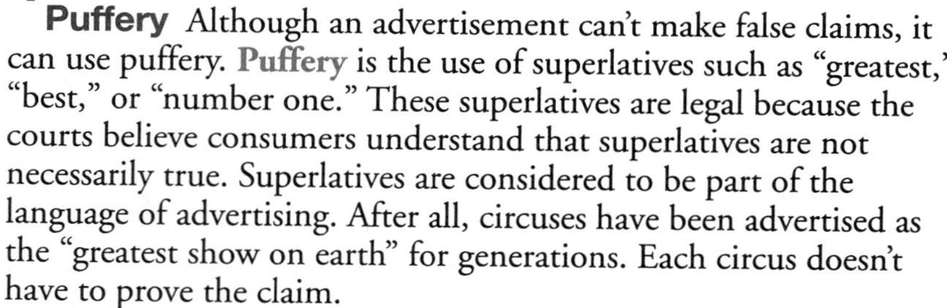

Puffery Although an advertisement can't make false claims, it can use puffery. **Puffery** is the use of superlatives such as "greatest," "best," or "number one." These superlatives are legal because the courts believe consumers understand that superlatives are not necessarily true. Superlatives are considered to be part of the language of advertising. After all, circuses have been advertised as the "greatest show on earth" for generations. Each circus doesn't have to prove the claim.

Emotional Appeal Product advertising that appeals to your emotions is not illegal. A claim that a car is beautiful or enhances your prestige can't be measured. Your idea of beauty is unique to you. If the accuracy of a claim can't be measured, the claim can't be illegal or unethical.

ADVERTISING AIMED AT CHILDREN

Advertising that is aimed at children is a subject of many ethical debates. Children *are* consumers. When they see an advertisement for something they want, they can often convince a parent to buy the product. This fact reinforces business decisions to target children with advertisements.

On the other hand, children are not *educated* consumers. They have no concept of the value of money, the price of a toy, or the quality of the advertised product. They don't understand that the neat bendable part might break off easily, leaving the toy useless.

ETHICAL ADVERTISING

In the end, ethics in advertising is both a personal and a business decision. Remember, you, the consumer, are in charge.

What is puffery?

____

____

Have you seen children react to advertising? Describe their reactions and the advertisements that caught their attention. How did their reactions differ from yours?

THINK CRITICALLY

1. Were any government agencies established to regulate advertising? Explain your answer.

2. What organization helps the advertising industry to regulate itself?

3. Why isn't puffery illegal?

MAKE CONNECTIONS

4. **RESEARCH** Use the library or Internet. Select one of the regulatory acts that impacted advertising. Write a one-page description of the act and its impact.

5. **COMMUNICATION** Some people favor self-regulation. Some don't. Choose a side. Be prepared to debate the issue in class. Prepare a presentation defending one side of the issue.

6. **PROBLEM SOLVING** Ray Dazai is concerned about advertising aimed at teenagers. How would you set his mind at ease?

7. **SOCIAL STUDIES** Use the library or Internet. Write one page describing how another country regulates its advertising more or less than the United States.

REVIEW

CHAPTER SUMMARY

LESSON 2.1 Evolution of Advertising

A. Modern advertising has evolved steadily since 1704.

B. Future developments will include interactive media such as the Internet.

LESSON 2.2 Advertising Industry

A. The structure of the advertising industry includes advertisers, advertising agencies, external facilitators, and the media.

B. Forces creating change are new retail channels, market saturation, integrated marketing messages, and consolidation of media and business.

LESSON 2.3 Advertising Agencies

A. In-house agencies, creative boutiques, media-buying services, interactive agencies, and full-service agencies provide different services.

B. A full-service advertising agency provides various services—account, marketing, creative, production, media, and administrative.

LESSON 2.4 Regulations and Ethics

A. Several government agencies regulate the advertising industry.

B. The consumer must require ethical advertising.

VOCABULARY BUILDER

Choose the term that best fits the definition. Write the letter of the answer in the space provided. Some terms may not be used.

____ **1.** All marketing activities, such as advertising, sales promotions, event sponsorships, and public relations

____ **2.** The use of superlatives in advertising

____ **3.** An advertising department in a company whose main business is not advertising

____ **4.** An agency that specializes in developing creative concepts, writing creative text, and providing artistic services

____ **5.** Specializes in buying media time and space

____ **6.** A company made up of professionals who specialize in providing creative and business services involved in planning, preparing, and placing advertisements

____ **7.** Specialize in helping clients prepare advertising for new interactive media

____ **8.** Distinct group of productive or profit-making businesses

____ **9.** Individuals or companies that perform specialized services for advertisers and advertising agencies

a. advertising agency
b. creative boutique
c. external facilitators
d. full-service agency
e. in-house agency
f. industry
g. interactive agencies
h. marketing mix
i. media-buying service
j. puffery

REVIEW CONCEPTS

10. What are the three criteria that define an advertisement?

11. Why is traditional advertising considered to be passive?

12. What determines the amount of money a business will spend on advertising?

13. How does the current quantity of advertisements affect the industry?

14. What are the five types of advertising agencies?

15. Why are traffic managers important in the advertising process?

16. How can the Federal Communications Commission affect a station that airs obscenities?

17. What type of advertising does the U.S. Postal service regulate?

REVIEW

18. What does ethical behavior mean?

19. What is the role of the marketing services group in a full-service agency?

APPLY WHAT YOU LEARNED

20. How can you support ethics in advertising?

21. In which area of a full-service agency would you prefer to be employed? Why?

22. Do you think an in-house agency or an advertising agency would produce the best results for an advertiser? Explain.

23. How do you think advertisers will try to overcome the challenge of market saturation? Why?

24. Does this additional information about advertising affect your response to advertisements? Why or why not?

MAKE CONNECTIONS

25. GOVERNMENT Do you think advertisements aimed at children should be regulated differently than other advertisements? Write a letter to your government representative outlining your position.

26. PROBLEM SOLVING Which aspects of his sandwich shops do you think Ray Dazai should emphasize in the advertising campaign for Ray's Deli? Explain your answer.

____

____

____

27. RESEARCH Use the Internet. Look at the amount of advertising located on most web pages. Given the amount of advertising and the amount of people using the Internet, what argument could you make in favor of regulating it? What argument could you make against regulating advertising on the Internet?

____

____

____

____

____

28. SOCIAL STUDIES Use the library or Internet. China's economic system changed recently. Research how China regulates its advertising. How far has China come in regulating advertising? Write a brief paper about your findings.

29. SOCIAL STUDIES Write one page comparing the advertising regulations in the U.S. to those in China.

30. MATHEMATICS Contact a local advertising agency, or use the Internet. Compare the agency's method of determining fees to the commission method described in this chapter. Is it better, worse, or the same? Explain.

31. BUSINESS MATH Calculate the amount your agency would receive in commission if an advertiser planned to spend $250,000 in advertising using the commission method described in the chapter.

____

____

____

____

____

CHAPTER 3

CAREERS IN ADVERTISING

UNITED AIRLINES

United Airlines is among the largest air carriers in the world. United flies to about 135 destinations in 26 countries. United Airlines had almost 1,000 full-time employees in 2000, before it bought out U.S. Airways. Most of United's employees are involved in flying or maintaining its fleet of airplanes or servicing its customers—pilots, flight attendants, customer service or reservation agents, and mechanics. Employees also fill management and other nonunion positions.

The Database Marketing Specialist develops and maintains the process for evaluating the direct response initiatives for Mileage Plus, a frequent flier program that provides incentives for customers to fly on United Airlines. Initiatives include mail, e-mail, newspapers, and newsletters.

This position requires a bachelor of science degree and a background in mathematics/statistics, at least two years of experience in direct marketing, experience in data analysis, and project management skills.

THINK CRITICALLY

1. Why would data be so valuable to a company like United Airlines?
2. What kind of experience can qualify you for this position?

ANALYZE YOUR CUSTOMERS

LESSONS

3.1 UNDERSTAND THE CONSUMER

3.2 TARGET THE CONSUMER

3.3 TEST THE MESSAGE

The Chapter 3 video for this module introduces the concepts in this chapter.

PROJECT

Market Research for a New Service

PROJECT OBJECTIVES

- Use the research process to decide if a new service would be marketable
- Select and describe the target segment for the product and advertising
- Create a positioning strategy
- Create an advertisement based on the target segment and positioning strategy
- Test the effectiveness of your advertisement

GETTING STARTED

Read through the Project Process below. Make a list of any materials you will need. Decide how you will get the needed materials or information.

- The Home Technology Store plans to start a service that sets up and services computers bought at Home Technology and other stores. The company believes home users need help setting up and maintaining their computers.
- Bring in advertising for related fields, such as computer service.
- List the media options for your ad. Which will reach your target segment?

PROJECT PROCESS

Part 1 **LESSON 3.1** Describe the culture, values, social class, community, and gender of your potential customer. Identify the benefits of the service that might attract consumers and influence their purchasing decisions.

Part 2 **LESSON 3.2** Choose a target segment and positioning strategy, including all the points described in the text. Create information if you don't have information readily available. Mock up an advertisement that uses your positioning strategy that you believe will reach the target segment.

Part 3 **LESSON 3.3** Select one of the test methods to follow when you present your mock advertisement. Prepare a prerelease for your advertisement. Decide which kind of prerelease test you will conduct.

CHAPTER REVIEW

Project Wrap-up Tell the class about the target segment. Ask them to think like the target segment when they view the advertisement. Follow the test method you selected. Present the advertisement, and collect the feedback.

LESSON 3.1

UNDERSTAND THE CONSUMER

EXPLAIN the factors that identify a consumer

DESCRIBE the consumer's decision-making process

IDENTIFY THE CONSUMER

How do you identify yourself? Your identity may include your name, your nationality, and your gender. You may also identify yourself by your favorite color, your taste in music, the length of your hair, and your profession or hobbies. Advertisers are interested in all of these characteristics that make you unique. Why are they interested?

Advertisers use this information to sell more. An advertisement must make a connection with you to be successful. To make the connection, an advertiser must understand your motives and priorities. Although motives, priorities, and values are all very personal, many of your personal characteristics are similar to others in your family, gender, or community. Therefore, advertisers can use information about the larger groups to target a smaller group of consumers.

ON THE $CENE

Rita Patel wants to open a company that will make simple home-cooked meals of four to eight servings. These meals would be ordered at least a day in advance. She plans to deliver the meals to any house on her side of town. Before she starts her business, she wants to research the potential market. What steps would you recommend?

CULTURE

Culture is an integrated pattern of behavior, knowledge, and beliefs that are acquired from a group and passed on to future generations. Culture includes large items, such as your values, and small details, such as what you eat and how you hold your fork to eat.

Culture affects what you think of yourself and others, as well as what they think of you. It affects all of your behavior, including what you buy, how you pay for it, and the value you put on it.

Individuals visiting from a different culture often look out of place. In the same way, advertisements that don't fit into your culture also look out of place. Advertisers must stay within your cultural boundaries to make a connection with you. This is especially important when advertising in foreign countries. If an advertisement does not fit into your culture, it quickly will be rejected, and the message will be ignored.

Values and Rituals Many of your values are a result of your culture. The importance you place on values such as cleanliness, individuality, and honesty are learned as part of your culture. An advertisement that rejects the values of a culture will be rejected by that culture. It may offend or anger members of the culture. It may even offend the consumers that the advertisement was meant to influence in a positive way.

A **ritual** is a formalized act or series of acts that is performed frequently. Rituals often reflect the values of a culture. For example, the Thanksgiving and Fourth of July holidays are full of rituals that reinforce the American values of freedom and individuality. Daily rituals also reflect your cultural values. An activity as simple as brushing your teeth is a daily ritual that reflects the value your culture places on cleanliness.

Products that fit into an existing ritual have a better chance of success than a product that is not part of any ritual. Unassociated products face the challenging, expensive, and often impossible task of proving their value to consumers.

SOCIAL CLASS

A **social class** is a group sharing the same economic or social status. Class membership is based on many factors. The most important factors include income, education, and occupation. A higher social class implies higher income, more education, and a more prestigious occupation. In America, social classes are not well defined, and individuals can move from one class to another. Most upward moves require an increase in one of the three most important factors.

Members of a social class live in similar houses, think in similar ways, and purchase similar items. Drive through any neighborhood. Notice the similarities in the size of the houses, house and yard maintenance, cars, and satellite or antennae usage. Most differences you notice usually will be minor. In fact, if you detect more important differences, the residents may be ready for a change in social class.

The size of the American middle class is shrinking. From 1994 to 2000, 4.4 percent of the households in America moved from the middle class to the upper income level. In 2000, more than 20 percent of households earned more than $75,000.

More importantly, members of the same social class are exposed to the same advertising because they use similar media. They read similar magazines and watch the same television shows. Many advertisers think that social class is one of the best indicators of potential customers.

COMMUNITY

A **community** is a group of people with a common characteristic or interest living within a larger society. Communities can be based on where you live, such as a neighborhood. They can also be based on or include a common characteristic, such as age or employment status of the inhabitants in a retirement community.

Individuals do not have to live near one another in order to be a community. A community can be made up of individuals connected only by a common interest, such as collecting baseball cards or restoring classic cars. Today communities based on mutual interest can live in different cities, states, even countries. They can communicate through media such as magazines, web sites, and newsletters delivered electronically or through the mail.

WORKSHOP

Identify your place in each of these groups. Do you belong to more than one community? What interests or common characteristics tie you to other members of the community?

FAMILY

The family unit is a group of consumers. It is difficult to explain or even anticipate the roles played by individual family members in making purchasing decisions. Although young children do not make the decisions, they are the reason for many purchases. Parents often overlap in decision-making responsibilities.

Advertisers can tell a lot about the needs of family when they know the age of the youngest child in the family. This identifies the type of products the family will buy, the income they need to save, and even the vacations the family might plan.

When children leave home and begin to shop for themselves, they will often buy the same products and brands their parents bought. Following their parents' purchase patterns provides some security for the newly independent household. In this way, brand loyalty can be passed from one generation to the next. You buy a certain brand of detergent, pudding, or batteries because you remember those brands from your parents' home.

GENDER

Gender is an obvious factor in consumption. However, differences in consumption are not well defined. In fact, advertisers present images that help to define the role of gender in purchasing their products. Advertisers can get into trouble, though, if they present images that are insulting or offensive. Remember, messages that are outside of a consumer's view of the world will be rejected.

Which group do advertisers think is one of the best indicators of potential customers?

____

____

MAKE A PURCHASING DECISION

Every time you purchase a product, you follow a sequence of steps. The amount of time you spend on each step varies. It depends on the complexity of the product and the importance you place on the item.

THE DECISION-MAKING PROCESS

The time you spend on this process depends on the complexity of the decision. Buying a pack of gum can be a quick, impulsive decision that happens in less than a minute while you stand in the checkout lane. Buying a house can take days, weeks, or longer. The process of making a purchasing decision occurs in six steps. Advertising can play a role in each step. The steps involve identifying a need or problem, identifying the choices, evaluating the choices, choosing one, acting on your choice, and reviewing your decision.

Step 1 Define the Problem After the basic needs for food, clothes, and shelter have been satisfied, any group you participate in or advertisements you see can affect or create wants. The wants are the problem you try to solve.

Groups can drive wants. For example, a group consisting of students has specific wants. Smaller groups identify more specific wants. Although they are all students, the wants of a child in grade school are very different from the wants of a high school student, a college student, or a student enrolled in continuing education classes. The wants of someone who creates stained glass windows are different from the wants of an accountant even though they are both professionals.

Advertisements can also create wants. Have you ever headed into the kitchen for a snack after watching a food commercial on television? An effective advertisement for a product can inspire you to think, "That would be great! I *want* that." Five minutes before the advertisement, you would never have thought of *wanting* the product.

Step 2 Identify the Choices Identifying a need or want sets the decision-making process in motion. Next, you will look for a way to satisfy your need or want.

Advertising is a critical part of this step. You will remember or notice advertisements for products that could satisfy your need or want. For example, if you recognize a need to prepare for winter, you will probably notice advertisements for snow tires, winter clothes, and sport utility vehicles with four-wheel drive. You might also notice advertisements for hot chocolate, hot soup, and vacations in Tahiti.

Before you search for information, you will recall anything you already know. Sometimes that is enough. Simple consumer decisions can be made quickly without additional research.

If the product is complex and is not part of your personal experience, you will need to spend more time searching for more information. This could include looking up product reviews on the Internet or in consumer publications, talking with people who already own the product, and examining the product.

Step 3 Evaluate the Choices After searching for information, you must evaluate it. Some information may have come from consumer organizations, and some information may have come from a product's advertising. You must take into account that these different sources may have some bias. For example, a consumer organization may have a certain advertiser as a sponsor. This organization may be hesitant to give the sponsor's product a bad review. Also, advertising from the company that produces a product probably won't show you a completely accurate picture of the advantages and disadvantages of the product. Advertisers pay big money to show a product in the most favorable light.

Step 4 Choose One After you identify your need or want and you identify and evaluate all your alternatives, you have a strong foundation for making an informed decision. A decision is made.

Step 5 Act on Your Choice At this point, you've made your choice. You step up to the counter and pay for the product. Theoretically, the advertiser has succeeded.

Step 6 Review Your Decision After your money has moved into the advertiser's pocket, the advertiser assumes that if you have bought a certain product, you will probably buy a similar product again. This includes small items, such as hot chocolate, and large items, such as cars or houses. Also, after you own a product, your opinion could become important to someone else searching for information about purchasing the product.

This makes the time after your purchase very important to advertisers. They want you to feel good about your decision and satisfied with the product. Reinforcement after the purchase can include direct mail or other forms of contact. After you make a major purchase, a sales representative will often contact you by telephone to offer assistance or answer questions. Most warranty cards require the consumer to give information about themselves and their buying decisions. Surveys may ask you to rate the quality of your contact with the company and ask for suggestions about improving future contacts.

Some companies may offer you a small fee or discount on your service rates if you refer new customers to them. Car dealerships may offer a discount on maintenance if you have your car serviced there. This increases the possibility that you might purchase your next car at the same location. For the same reason, they may send you tips about using the model you purchased and information about upgrades or new models as they are produced.

What do you do after you recognize a need or want?

____

____

THINK CRITICALLY

1. How will an individual respond to an advertisement that does not fit into his or her culture?

2. What impact does a ritual have on a new product?

3. What characteristics can be a basis for a community?

4. How long does the process of making a purchasing decision take?

5. What impact can advertising have on your wants?

MAKE CONNECTIONS

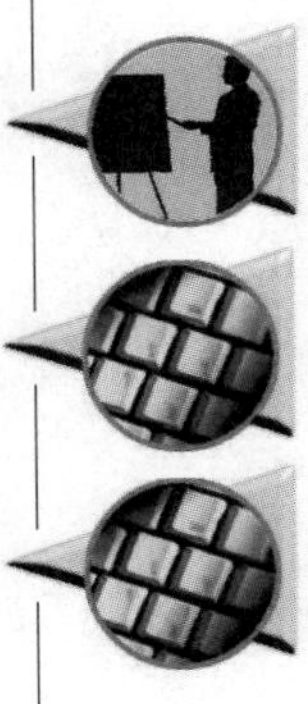

6. **HISTORY** Using the library or Internet, look up the development of social classes in the United States. Has the definition of each class changed over time? Prepare a presentation on your findings.

7. **PROBLEM SOLVING** What advertising media would you recommend to reach everyone in your neighborhood? Write one page to explain your recommendation.

8. **COMMUNICATION** Clip an advertisement in a publication. Who was the target of the advertisement? How can you tell? Write a one-page paper describing the items that identify the target.

LESSON 3.2
TARGET THE CONSUMER

DESCRIBE market segmentation

DIFFERENTIATE between the positioning strategies

DETERMINE THE MARKET SEGMENT

Consumers belong to a variety of groups based on criteria such as location, gender, and common interests. These groups influence the needs, wants, and consumer behavior of every individual in the group.

Advertisers also break consumers into groups based on a variety of criteria. Some of the criteria are the same as those that determine the consumer groups.

Advertisers must determine who should view their advertisements and what the advertisements should say to reach the consumer. Therefore, the groups assigned by advertisers are very specific. These groups are target segments. A **target segment** is a subgroup of the market chosen to be the focus of the marketing and advertising campaign.

ON THE $CENE

Rita's company, "What's Cooking," makes simple home-cooked meals of four to eight servings. She has an established list of regular clients, and more call every day. Because she has so much business, she is moving to a commercial building and hiring more cooks and drivers. Before she starts to advertise, she needs to identify her target segment. What would you recommend?

DEFINE A MARKET SEGMENT

An advertiser divides the entire market into smaller submarkets called **market segments**. A market segment is a group of people with common characteristics and similar needs and wants.

In order to segment a market, the market must be large enough to divide, be accessible to advertisers, and have distinct characteristics that can be used to create segments. If a product appeals to only 500 people, there is no point in segmenting the market. If advertisers cannot reach the group, there is no point in creating advertising that the group will not be able to view. Finally, if there are no differences between group members, there is no basis that can be used to create the segments.

Five of the most common methods used to create market segments are demographics, usage and commitment, geography, psychographics, and benefits. Regardless of the method, two factors must be present in each segment.

1. The members of the segment must have common characteristics that will cause them to respond to a marketing program in a similar way.
2. The same media must reach all the members of the segment.

Demographics The statistical characteristics of human populations are **demographics**. Demographics include information such as age, race, gender, income, marital status, education, and occupation. It is common to combine demographics with one of the other market segmentation methods to identify target segments. For example, new consumers also share certain demographics of age (18–25), marital status, and so on. This helps an advertiser target the group more specifically. The more specific the definition of the target segment, the better chance the advertiser will have of connecting successfully to the consumer.

The U.S. Census Bureau collects demographic data. This information is very useful to businesses. In addition to other functions, it can be used to determine the size of the potential market for a new product.

For example, Air Ticket, a small airline company, wants to calculate the possible gross profit and net profit from a promotion aimed at elderly Americans. To qualify, passengers must be age 65 or older. According to the Census Bureau, there are 31,241,831 Americans 65 or older. Air Ticket plans to offer a round-trip ticket for $125 to any city in the United States. The advertising campaign will cost $2,750,000. What is the possible gross profit and net profit if 10% of the market buys tickets?

SOLUTION

10% of 31,241,831 = 3,124,183

Tickets × Price = Gross profit
3,124,183 × $125 = Gross profit
$390,522,875 = Gross profit

Gross Profit − Expenses = Net profit
$390,522,875 − $2,750,000 = Net profit
$387,772,875 = Net profit

Air Ticket is anticipating almost $400 million in net profit.

List several products. Identify your usage or commitment level for each product. How could an advertiser persuade you to buy a different product?

Advertisers find demographics very useful in choosing the media to reach a target segment. Characteristics such as age, income, occupation, and gender will often identify a common method of communication, such as magazines or radio stations.

Usage and Commitment Usage level and commitment to the product are common methods of segmenting markets. For some products and services, heavy users are responsible for the majority of sales. Therefore, they are often the primary target segment. The disadvantage of this theory is that heavy users may not need encouragement to buy the product. By concentrating on the heavy users, the advertiser is losing the opportunity to encourage other segments to buy the product.

Usage and Commitment	Cost and Impact
Nonuser	Most difficult to persuade
Switcher—purchases based on sales or incentives	Expensive to persuade and difficult to keep
New consumer	Low short-term return, but could create brand-loyal users in the future
Brand-loyal consumer	Difficult to convert
Heavy user	May not need persuasion

Geography Market segmentation based on geographic location is also common. Consumers who live near each other share a variety of characteristics. Culture, values, and recreational activities are affected by your geographic location. If you live in Colorado, you are more likely to ski than to surf. Even the foods you prefer and the foods available to you are affected by your geographic location.

Combining demographics with geographic market segmentation can provide a very strong method of identifying a specific target market. The combination can provide a common contact method for advertisers. Local media, sorted by demographic appeal, can be identified easily for the target segment.

Psychographics Advertisers created the psychographics category to describe a market segmentation method that concentrates on the consumer's activities, interests, and opinions. Advertisers who make a connection by reflecting a consumer's lifestyle create messages that seem valid to the target market.

Insight into your motivation enables advertisers to understand the reasons for your behavior. After they understand your motivation, they can apply it to any number of products. If you are constantly looking for ways to save time, you might eat fast food, buy frozen meals, use drive-through banking services, and choose a store based on its convenient location.

Benefits Benefit segmentation creates segments based on the benefit packages that different customers want from the same category. For example, consumers want different benefits from purchasing a house. Some people want a large house. Others want a smaller, more comfortable home. Some houses differ in location, such as subdivisions or rural or urban settings. Each consumer would be drawn to a different type of advertisement.

SELECT A TARGET

After the market segments have been established, the advertiser can select one or more of the market segments to become the target segments. Before choosing a target market, the advertiser must take a long look at its own advantages and disadvantages. Choosing the wrong target can have disastrous results.

Perhaps Widgets, Inc., could sell a million widgets, but if it doesn't have the manufacturing resources to make a million widgets, its customers may become dissatisfied. Dissatisfaction can cause a company to lose customers quickly.

Regardless of how the market is segmented, each segment will have a different level of appeal to the advertiser. The advertiser must use several criteria to select the best target segments.

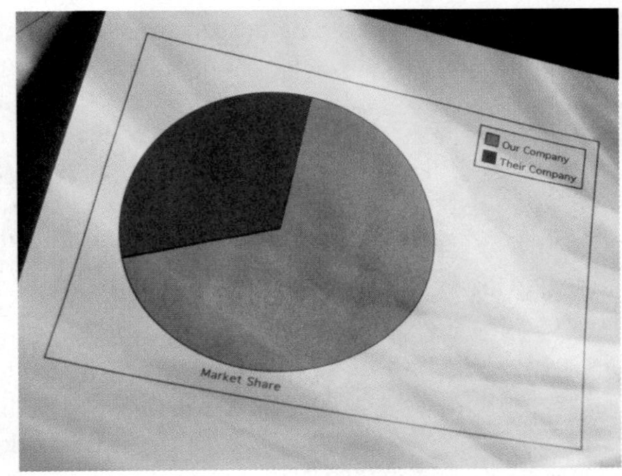

1. ***Current size of the market*** Is the current target market for the product too big or too small? If it's too big, the advertiser won't be able to meet the demand. If the market is too small, it might not be worth the advertiser's time and money.
2. ***Expected growth of the market segment*** If the current market is the right size, will it continue to grow? Can the advertiser keep up with the market's growth? Can the advertiser influence the growth of the market segment through advertising?
3. ***Cost of reaching the segment*** How much will it cost to reach the market segment through advertising? Is the profit worth the cost?
4. ***Compatibility with the advertiser's objectives and resources*** Do the market segment's characteristics fit into the advertiser's plans for its future? Do the values of the segment fit into the advertiser's corporate image? Does the advertiser have the resources available to make, ship, and sell the product? Will it be necessary to increase manufacturing capabilities or personnel?

What five common methods are used to create market segments?

CHOOSE A POSITIONING STRATEGY

The process of making an advertiser's product different from other products in the consumer's mind is **positioning**. The real difference between one package of paper plates and the package right next to it on the shelf is probably minor. You might choose the second package only because of the differences you remember from the television commercial you saw several times in the past week. As you toss the package into the cart, you don't realize that the advertiser's positioning strategy was successful.

ESSENTIAL ELEMENTS OF A POSITIONING STRATEGY

Positioning strategies provide consumers with reasons to purchase specific products. To be effective, a positioning strategy must have the elements of substance, consistency, and a simple, distinctive theme.

Substance For a positioning strategy to remain effective over time, it must be backed by substance. If a restaurant claims to have fast, friendly service, it must back the claim with service that really is fast and friendly. If it doesn't, the campaign will fail. When you find slow and unfriendly service at the restaurant, you won't return for another visit.

Consistency The advertising message must be consistent internally and over time. Internally everything must work together to reinforce the message. The restaurant must purchase equipment to heat the meals quickly. It must hire enough people to clear the tables and take orders quickly.

Consistency over time requires that the advertiser send the same simple message day after day. Even though the individual advertisements will change, the basic message must be the same. This message becomes the theme of the campaign.

ADVERTISING GLOBALLY

Foreign companies can succeed in Japan if they do a little research first. Companies that don't do their homework fail. For example, a carpetmaker tried to sell carpets that were too big for Japanese houses. After research, companies such as Levi-Strauss designed products for the Japanese market. Levi-Strauss made a special line of jeans in Japanese sizes.

THINK CRITICALLY Why is research important when moving into foreign markets?

Simple, Distinctive Theme You must understand what a product can do before you will buy it. A complicated message won't be understood or remembered by the audience.

POSITIONING THEMES

A positioning theme creates a focus for the advertising campaign and helps an advertiser make internal decisions that create substance for the customer. It should be short, to the point, and easy to remember. Select a single idea as the focus. If more than one idea is selected, the message may become confusing or lack focus.

Positioning themes can be physical or perceptual. Physical positioning strategies emphasize the objective physical characteristics of the product. A car can go from 0 to 60 miles per hour in a few seconds. The air bags deploy when the car collides with an object at 25 miles per hour. Perceptual positioning strategies emphasize emotional or subjective opinions about the product. A car is exciting or safe or adds to the owner's status.

There are several basic themes an advertiser might select. The advertiser can choose physical or perceptual characteristics within each theme.

Benefit Positioning Advertisers should select only a single benefit that is important to the consumer. Placing the focus on the benefit will interest consumers searching for that feature. If you are looking for a car that is reliable, advertisements that emphasize low maintenance needs will interest you. If you want a car that is safe, advertisements that emphasize the car's safety record or safety features will attract you.

User Positioning Rather than focusing on anything about the product, user positioning focuses on the user. This is common when the target segment has been chosen using demographic and psychographics criteria that have revealed a fairly complete picture of the target's lifestyle. The advertisements show how the product fits into that lifestyle.

Competitive Positioning Competitive positioning is useful to make sure a product stands out in a crowded product market. Smaller companies use this method to carve out part of the larger market for their products. Competitive positioning must emphasize the difference between your product and similar products on the shelf.

REPOSITIONING

An advertising campaign doesn't always live up to expectations the first time. There are various reasons. The market changes constantly. The competitor may have reacted differently than expected, or the consumer's preferences may have changed. Regardless, it may be necessary to start over. Repositioning is always a special challenge, but adapting assures the campaign will remain relevant.

What elements must a positioning strategy have to be effective?

____

____

Suppose you work for a small advertising agency. You have been asked to analyze a new product for students. The product automatically calculates a current grade in each class based on grades the students have received on assignments and tests. List several physical and perceptual benefits. Create a positioning theme for two of the benefits. Which theme is better? Why?

THINK CRITICALLY

1. Why are demographics useful in choosing the media to reach a target segment?

2. Why can psychographics be applied to more than one product?

3. What are the five levels of usage and commitment?

4. What are the essential elements of a positioning strategy?

5. Why would it be necessary to reposition?

MAKE CONNECTIONS

6. **COMMUNICATION** Suppose you own five gift shops. Your recent advertising campaign directed at young professionals did not have the impact you expected. Write a letter to your advertising agency. Do you think repositioning would be a good idea? If so, suggest a new position.

7. **PROBLEM SOLVING** Suppose you own a major airline. The proposed positioning strategy is "On time. Every time." Your record for on-time departures and arrivals isn't the best. What kind of changes would you have to make?

LESSON 3.3
TEST THE MESSAGE

GOALS

DESCRIBE the role of research before an advertisement is released

DISTINGUISH between the methods used to evaluate an advertisement's potential impact

THE ROLE OF RESEARCH

You have probably seen a commercial that was so funny you laughed out loud when you were sitting alone in front of the television. It was so funny and so true that you wanted to share it with someone. Advertisers knew you would be watching and that the commercial would reflect your experience accurately. Commercials like that happen because advertisers did their research.

ADVERTISING RESEARCH

Advertising research is the thorough investigation of the planning, preparation, and placement of advertisements. Research should happen several times at different points in the process of creating an advertisement.

ON THE $CENE

Rita's company, "What's Cooking," wasn't growing as fast as she hoped after opening a commercial kitchen. The advertising agency created a survey she could give to her current clients. The responses indicated that her present clients are happy. She needs more clients to support the cost of the kitchen and employees. Can you suggest any immediate ways of getting more clients? What kind of research would help her?

1. ***Select the target segment.*** Research will help the advertiser determine who will buy the product.
2. ***Understand the target segment before creating the advertising.*** To create a connection between the advertiser and the consumer, advertising must accurately reflect the target segment's world.
3. ***Evaluate the advertisement's effectiveness before it is released to the media.*** After the advertisement is developed, present it to test audiences in several ways. The response of the test audience will predict the results when the message is released. If the message does not get the response the advertiser wants, changes can be made until it tests successfully.
4. ***Evaluate the advertisement's remaining effectiveness before it is withdrawn from the media.*** Even the best advertisement loses its effectiveness as time passes. It may be funny the first time you see it. You'll still laugh after seeing it a number of times, but eventually you won't notice it when you see it. It's time to withdraw the advertisement.

DEVELOPMENTAL RESEARCH

Developmental advertising research helps to create the advertising message by providing several important pieces of information. Many advertisers believe that the research at this point in the creation process may be the most important.

Idea Generation Customer contact is a great way to get new, original ideas for advertising. Talk to members of the target segment. Ask them why they would want to buy the product. Their answers might give the advertising agency some completely new ideas about presenting the product.

Environmental Analysis Your environment changes daily. Environmental analysis evaluates the potential influence of your environment, including social and cultural trends, economics, and politics. This defines the context in which you will send or receive the message. Your world must be pictured accurately to make a connection.

Audience Definition Get to know the target segment. An advertiser who really knows the audience can present a message that is meaningful to the targeted consumer. This will also help advertisers choose the best media to reach the target segment most efficiently.

Audience Profiling This is one of the most important research areas for creating and developing the advertisement. Lifestyle research, surveys, and in-depth interviews can provide a complete picture of the individual consumer to the creative staff. This will help them create an advertisement that fits the target audience.

When should research first enter the advertising process?

____

____

EVALUATE THE IMPACT

When you talk with your friends, you can tell when they really understand what you are saying. You can also tell when they entirely miss the point.

Evaluating the impact of an advertising message is similar. You ask questions, you judge the audience's interest level, and you watch their behavior. There are many ways of doing this. Some involve close contact with members of a test group, while others are simple impersonal questions that can be answered on paper rather than in person. A *prerelease test* is done before the advertisement is placed in the media. A *posttest* is conducted after the advertisement is placed in the media.

WHAT CAN YOU MEASURE?

Before you can test, you have to know what kind of information you want to collect. Usually the account team and client want to know that the advertisement will have the right effect. This can be discovered in a prerelease test.

An advertisement must accomplish several things to be effective. Measuring the advertisement's success or failure in these areas will provide an accurate test of the advertisement's effectiveness. The message should provide information, affect the audience's attitude, attach emotions, and validate a brand.

Provide Knowledge The intent of most advertising is to give the audience information. It can be as simple as retaining a brand name. Recall and recognition tests will tell the advertiser how much the audience remembers. Sometimes an advertisement can be too catchy. For example, people may remember the advertisement but not the company or product.

Shape Attitude A preference or an attitude is an evaluation caused by several factors. If an advertisement can change your opinion about one of the factors, it might also affect your opinion of the product.

READ A CONSUMER'S MIND DURING ADS The technology to accurately read a consumer's response to advertisements and media messages is nearing completion. There is a headset that allows advertisers to read a consumer's brain-wave activity to see which messages are impacting the consumer. The headset reads electrical signals from the scalp five times per second while the subject views the advertisement. The brain waves are converted to a graph synchronized with the advertisement. The advertiser has a play-by-play record of images that excite the subject and those that don't. The new device is based on electroencephalogram technology developed by NASA to monitor the alertness levels of astronauts. Capita Research Group is developing the commercial application for this technology.

THINK CRITICALLY Is this an improvement over methods such as surveys or focus groups? Explain your answer. What are the advantages and disadvantages of this method?

Describe an event that happened to you. Tell it once without any emotional descriptive terms. Tell it a second time with emotionally descriptive phrases. Which is more memorable? Why?

Attach Emotions The importance of emotion in advertisements is debated. However, an advertisement that affects your emotions is easier to remember than an advertisement with no emotional impact at all.

Validate a Brand It is important for an advertisement to feel true to the target audience. Advertisements that feel true to the audience will create a connection to the product.

THE FOCUS GROUP—A DEVELOPMENTAL RESEARCH TOOL

A **focus group** consists of six to twelve consumers, led by a professional moderator, who discuss the product. Focus groups obtain in-depth information, but the number of consumers is very limited. The group represents only a small sample of the target segment. To be effective, the group must be led by an experienced moderator to keep the group on track and prevent domination by a single member.

PRERELEASE TEST METHODS

After the advertising message has been developed, most advertisers will test the message before it is released to the media. This prevents an expensive mistake and protects them from presenting the wrong image of their company or product. There are many ways of testing the message before it is released.

Communication Tests This tests the message the audience receives against the message the advertiser wants to send. This protects the advertiser from making an error in images or dialogue that would offend the audience.

Magazine Dummies A mock-up magazine is prepared with the advertisement. The test audience receives and reads the magazine at home. After they finish the magazine, they answer questions about the content and the advertisements. This tests recall and feelings about the advertisement.

Theater Tests Advertisements can be viewed in small theaters, usually near malls. This method is very popular, but it is often hard to tell if the audience reacts to the advertisement or the product.

Thought Listings After viewing the advertisement, small groups write down the thoughts they had during the advertisement. These responses can be measured in many ways. For example, common phrases or agreement with the message can be counted and interpreted.

PILOT TEST

Advertisements can be released to a small portion of the target segment before they are fully released. This is an option with most media. Broadcasts can be limited to areas. Magazines can be printed so only a percentage of the readers receive the ad. Direct mail can be sent to limited areas.

How important is emotion in advertising?

____

____

THINK CRITICALLY

1. What do advertisers gain by researching to understand the target audience?

2. Why should an advertiser test the message on an audience before releasing it?

3. How does an advertiser test the audience to verify that the product information was successfully learned?

4. Why is it important for an advertisement to feel true to the target audience?

MAKE CONNECTIONS

5. **RESEARCH** Use the library or Internet. Locate other methods of testing an advertising method. Write a one-page description of a method you locate.

6. **COMMUNICATION** Create a chart of the testing methods. Include advantages and disadvantages for each test method.

7. **PROBLEM SOLVING** A small client without a lot of money is evaluating the expense of testing an advertisement. Would you recommend testing or not? Explain your answer.

REVIEW

CHAPTER SUMMARY

LESSON 3.1 Understand the Consumer

A. Consumers can be defined by factors such as culture, social class, community, family, and gender.

B. Consumers follow a decision process that can be influenced by advertising.

LESSON 3.2 Target the Consumer

A. Every consumer belongs to a market segment that can be determined by the advertiser.

B. Positioning strategies are selected to make the advertiser's product different from other products.

LESSON 3.3 Test the Message

A. Research before an advertisement is released helps to create the message.

B. Several methods are used before an advertisement is released to evaluate its potential impact.

VOCABULARY BUILDER

Choose the term that best fits the definition. Write the letter of the answer in the space provided. Some terms may not be used.

____ **1.** Consists of six to twelve consumers and a professional moderator who discuss the product

____ **2.** Group of people with a common characteristic or interest living within a larger society

____ **3.** Process of making an advertiser's product different from other products in the consumer's mind

____ **4.** Statistical characteristics of human populations

____ **5.** Subgroup of the market chosen to be the focus of the marketing and advertising campaign

____ **6.** Formalized act or series of acts that is performed frequently

____ **7.** Integrated pattern of behavior, knowledge, and beliefs that are acquired from a group and passed on to future generations

____ **8.** Group of customers with common characteristics

____ **9.** Thorough investigation of the planning, preparation, and placement of advertisements

____ **10.** Group sharing the same economic or social status

a. advertising research
b. community
c. culture
d. demographics
e. focus group
f. market segment
g. positioning
h. ritual
i. social class
j. target segment

REVIEW CONCEPTS

11. Why are rituals important?

____

____

____

12. How do you move into a higher social class?

____

____

____

13. How is brand loyalty passed from one generation to the next?

____

____

____

14. What are the steps in making a purchasing decision?

____

____

____

15. What characteristics does a market need before it can be segmented?

____

____

____

16. What factors must be present in each market segment?

____

____

____

17. How does an advertiser show consistency over time?

____

____

____

18. When is it time to withdraw an advertisement?

____

____

____

POINT YOUR BROWSER
b2000.swep.com

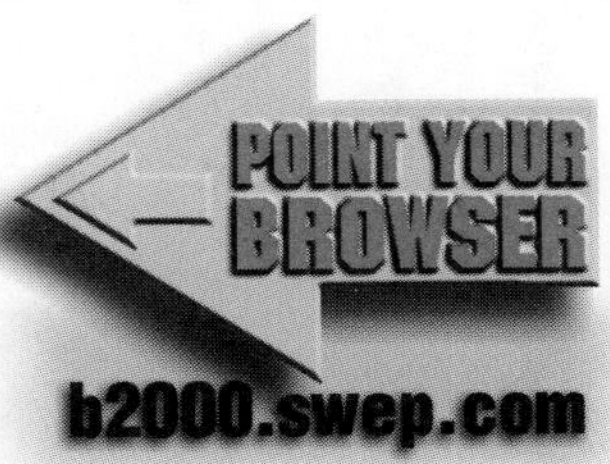

REVIEW

19. What is a good source of advertising ideas?

20. What is a preference?

APPLY WHAT YOU LEARNED

21. How has your culture affected your consumer behavior?

22. Why is it difficult to convert a brand-loyal consumer?

23. How would choosing a target market that is too small affect an advertiser?

24. Why does an advertiser consider the values of the target segment?

25. How would a company use advertising to improve its corporate image?

26. Advertisers spend a lot of money pretesting an advertising message. Do you think this is money well spent? Why or why not?

MAKE CONNECTIONS

27. **GOVERNMENT** Do you think the government should monitor the way companies use information they collect from surveys or other customer feedback? Should companies be allowed to trade this information? Write a few paragraphs that are intended to persuade someone to agree with your opinion on this subject.

28. **BUSINESS** Why would a company choose a positioning strategy that required expensive changes inside the company?

29. **RESEARCH** Which method of testing messages is best before the messages are released? Explain your answer.

30. **SOCIAL STUDIES** Use the library or Internet. America has been called a "melting pot." Do any cultural influences remain from immigrant populations? Would these populations influence the way an advertising message is received? Write a one-page paper. Use at least one example.

31. **COMMUNICATION** Select a television commercial. List the elements that identify the target segment. Explain why the advertiser selected those elements.

32. **BUSINESS MATH** Suppose your greeting card company is considering a new line of pet-related cards for a certain city. Your demographic data states that there are 2,566 pet owners in the city. This is your target market. Your cards will cost $2.95 each, and expenses run $1.06 per card. If you anticipate that 20 percent of the pet owners in the city will buy one card, what is the possible gross profit and net profit?

CHAPTER 4

PLAN YOUR ADVERTISING CAMPAIGN

LESSONS

4.1 DEVELOP AN ADVERTISING PLAN

4.2 SET OBJECTIVES AND BUDGET

4.3 COMPLETE THE ADVERTISING PLAN

CAREERS IN ADVERTISING

COMMONHEALTH

CommonHealth is an advertising agency that specializes in providing services for healthcare companies. The client list includes companies such as Blue Cross/Blue Shield and Johnson & Johnson. CommonHealth is one of the largest ad agencies in the world that specializes in healthcare. A full-service agency, it has assisted clients in all advertising activities including traditional advertising and strategic planning. In 1999, CommonHealth had 878 employees and billed more than $1 billion.

The Senior Account Planner works with account and creative resources. Responsibilities include agency planning and research needs as well as direct contact with major healthcare clients. Preferred experience includes 3–5 years performing planning functions. However, experience in related categories such as senior account manager and strategy and focus development will be considered. Experience working with the healthcare industry is helpful. CommonHealth offers career growth opportunities and a competitive and comprehensive benefit package.

THINK CRITICALLY

1. Why does the agency specialize in advertising for a single industry?
2. What does the Senior Account Planner do in an ad campaign?

The Chapter 4 video for this module introduces the concepts in this chapter.

PROJECT

Advertising Plan For North Point Amusement Park

PROJECT OBJECTIVES

- Prepare a situational analysis for an advertising plan
- Create set objectives for an advertising plan
- Create a budget for an advertising plan
- Create a strategy for executing an advertising plan
- Select a method of measuring the success of an advertising plan

GETTING STARTED

Read through the Project Process below. Make a list of any materials you will need. Decide how you will get the needed materials or information.

- North Point Amusement Park is a large amusement park near your community. It draws customers from several nearby cities and Canada and travelers from all over the country. Its main attraction is a spectacular wooden roller coaster. Recently, it bought additional land, including a large pond. This summer, it will open a water park and a family campground using the pond and surrounding land.
- Bring in advertising for other amusement parks.

PROJECT PROCESS

Part 1 **LESSON 4.1** Perform a situational analysis for the park and your area. Discuss the park's history, the park's strengths and weaknesses, the target market, and the park's competition. Since the park is not real, you may have to create much of this information, based on a real amusement park.

Part 2 **LESSON 4.2** Write objectives for the plan, including the measurements you will use to determine if the ad was successful. Select a method to determine the budget, and decide on an amount. Write your rationale for the method you will use to determine the budget.

Part 3 **LESSON 4.3** Identify the strategies you will use to carry out this advertising plan. Who is your target market? How will you market the park? How will you position the park in the market? Finally, discuss what methods you will use to measure the objectives you set in Part 2.

CHAPTER REVIEW

Project Wrap-up Present your plan to the class. How do the plans from other groups differ? What differences did you notice in the situational analyses?

LESSON 4.1
DEVELOP AN ADVERTISING PLAN

IDENTIFY the components of an advertising plan

PERFORM a situational analysis for a product or service

THE ADVERTISING PLAN

You already made many decisions today. When the alarm went off this morning, you decided if you would get up or hit the snooze button. Later you decided what to wear and what to eat. These were small decisions.

There are also large decisions. Will you continue your education? If so, what type of degree do you want? What profession will you choose? Where will you work?

How do you make decisions? All of your decisions should fit into your plans. A plan is a method created to achieve a specific goal. Although each decision is not significant, several decisions form a pattern. The patterns must fit into your plans. It doesn't matter if you are late for work once. If you are repeatedly late, you may be put on probation rather than get the promotion you want. Each individual decision to be late meant that your overall plan failed.

ON THE $CENE

Raymond Navarro owns several small businesses that rent vacation equipment such as canoes, paddleboats, hiking and camping equipment, mountain bicycles, and scuba gear. The rental sites are scattered through Ohio, Kentucky, and Indiana. This year he is adding several houseboats to the rental equipment at a state park in Indiana. He plans to unite the businesses under one name and provide a single phone number that customers can use to reserve equipment at any business location. He has met with the Bright Ideas Advertising Agency several times. The agency is developing an advertising plan for him. What information does Bright Ideas need to create the plan?

PURPOSE OF AN ADVERTISING PLAN

An **advertising plan** describes the thinking and tasks needed to achieve a successful advertising campaign that fits into the advertiser's marketing strategy. The advertising plan gives you a solid foundation to make advertising decisions. Each decision you make while creating the campaign must fit into the advertising plan. Any decision that doesn't fit into the plan could contribute to its failure.

COMPONENTS OF AN ADVERTISING PLAN

Most plans include similar components. Plans may contain additional components that provide more specific information or place the same components in a different order. An agency uses the same components in all advertising plans, whether the product is lightbulbs or dog food. Agencies seldom change the structure of their advertising plans. Following the same structure every year enables agencies to compare plans from year to year. Components for a sample advertising plan include:

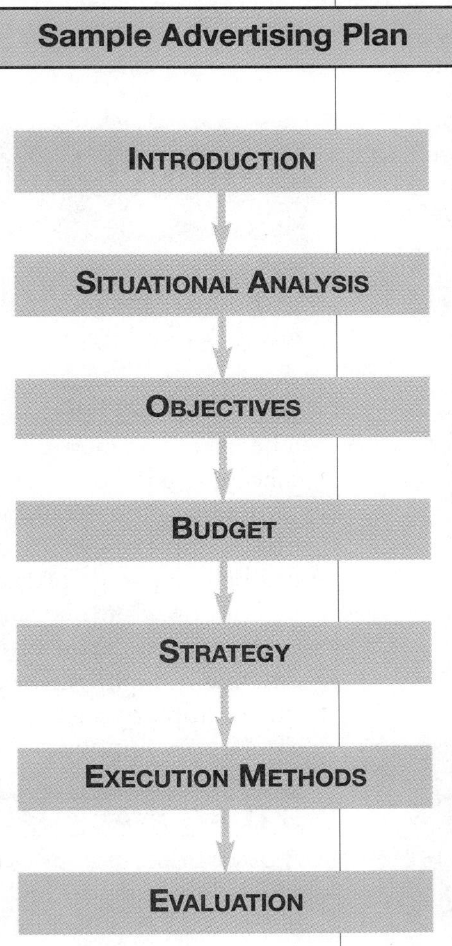

1. ***Introduction*** Presents an executive overview and summary of the entire plan.
2. ***Situational Analysis*** Describes the factors that influence the advertising plan.
3. ***Objectives*** Describes the goals that the advertising should accomplish.
4. ***Budget*** Identifies the amount of money that will be spent on advertising and the method used to calculate the amount.
5. ***Strategy*** Identifies how the advertising plan objectives will be accomplished.
6. ***Execution Methods*** Identifies where, when, and how the ad will be placed in the media.
7. ***Evaluation*** Describes the tests and criteria that will determine the success or failure of the advertising campaign.

MARKETING CONTEXT

An advertising plan is part of the marketing function. Any advertising should be directed by the marketing department and supported by its activities. For example, if your marketing department decides that a sale is necessary to increase consumer purchases, the advertising campaign should include sale information, coupons, or other supporting information.

Brand Image The *image* of a brand presented to consumers is decided by the marketing strategy. In fact, this is one of the most important strategic purposes of marketing. All marketing and advertising activities should work

List several brands that you frequently see advertised. What image do you think the advertisement is meant to project? How successful do you think the advertisers have been in presenting the image? How successful is the product?

together to present the desired image of the product. All advertisements in all media should present the same brand image. The same theme should be used in television advertisements, outdoor advertisements (billboards), magazine and print advertisements, Internet advertisements, and radio advertisements.

What is one of the most important strategic purposes of marketing?

____

____

INTRODUCTION AND SITUATIONAL ANALYSIS

The first two parts of the advertising plan are among the most important. Both are created by the agency and are based on information from the advertiser and research by the agency.

INTRODUCTION

The **executive summary** provides a summary of the most important information needed in order to make decisions concerning the advertising plan. It summarizes the detailed information found later in the document. The executive summary specifies the most important parts of the advertising plan and can be two paragraphs or two pages in length.

The **overview** identifies the document's structure and the material that will be covered in the advertising plan. The overview summarizes each part of the document, highlighting the important information in each section. The executive summary is similar to a summary of an entire book. The overview is similar to a summary of each chapter in the book.

SITUATIONAL ANALYSIS

A description of your current situation would include many items. Your personal circumstances include your age, your level of education, and your job or personal responsibilities. Your situation includes much more than that. Where do you live? Different communities, states, or countries all influence your habits, values, and opportunities. What is the current global situation? Is your country at war, involved in an internal political situation, or affected by drought? National factors can affect you as easily as the circumstances in your neighborhood. So many factors create your situation that it would be impossible to list all of them.

Just as a number of factors affect your situation, factors also affect the situation for the product in the advertising plan. A **situational analysis** is an examination of conditions and circumstances that affect the product or service. Because there are an infinite number of factors, you must select factors that have a significant impact on the product.

Overall, the situational analysis performs several functions.

1. Reviews the company and product history.
2. Evaluates the product's strengths and weaknesses.
3. Defines the target segment.
4. Evaluates the competition.

Demographics The most important factor described in an advertising plan may be demographics. Each generation has different needs. For example, the average age of Americans increases every year. Products for aging Americans will have a growing market in the near future.

Advertiser's History The advertiser's history of successes and failures will influence all of its decisions. It is also helpful for the agency to know the history of the advertiser, the industry, the brand, and the competition. Adding this information to the advertising plan proves to the advertiser that the agency has taken the time to become familiar with the advertiser.

Industry Analysis The advertiser's industry and the advertiser's status in the industry are very important. The **industry analysis** examines developments and trends in the industry. What advances have been made in the advertiser's field of business? Is the advertiser leading the field in technology, or will the company be left behind as the industry changes around it?

Market Analysis In the **market analysis**, the agency examines the customers and their motives for buying the product. The motivation of the current customers can help to identify and motivate new customers. The account services group in the agency can use this information to identify the benefits of the product and select the target segment.

Competitor Analysis The final piece of information is an analysis of the advertiser's competition. The **competitor analysis** examines the identity, strengths, and weaknesses of the competition and the competing product. This information is used to position the advertiser's product.

ADVERTISING GLOBALLY

The North American Free Trade Agreement (NAFTA) was implemented on January 1, 1994. It was designed to remove most obstacles that hindered trade between Mexico, Canada, and the United States. For example, all barriers, except tariffs, affecting agricultural trade between the U.S. and Mexico were dropped. Many other tariffs affecting trade between Mexico and the U.S. were scheduled to be dropped in the 5 to 15 years following the agreement. Most agricultural tariffs between Canada and the U.S. were removed by January 1, 1998. Canada and Mexico are the second and third largest export markets for American agricultural products. An increase in trade and the size of global markets creates a need for global advertising.

THINK CRITICALLY What is the benefit to U.S. agricultural producers?

Write an analysis of your current situation. Select factors from several levels that have an impact on your life. What factors do you have in common with other members of your class? What factors are unique to you?

GLOBAL SITUATIONAL ANALYSIS

Trade between countries is increasing, resulting in an increase in global advertising. Therefore, more factors must be considered in the situational analysis. Economic conditions in the country, demographics, and culture must be analyzed to determine the target segment, market size, and the way ads can form a connection with the consumers.

Economic Factors For most purposes, countries can be broken into two large groups based on economic development—developing countries and industrialized countries. Most developing countries are not good markets for consumer products. Most purchases will be business products, heavy machinery, and agricultural equipment used to improve the country's resources. Individual consumers will not be interested in products they can't use or don't need. A lamp may be a quality product, but it's useless in a village that does not have electricity. Industrial countries have well-established consumer markets. Analysis in these countries should include demographics and cultural differences that could affect the sale or use of the product.

Demographics Every country will have demographic characteristics that are unique to the population of that country. Demographics affect which products a population will buy and the advertising that will get a response from the consumers. Different countries also have different age characteristics. Although the average age of the American population is getting older, the average age of citizens in other countries is often younger. This affects the needs and wants of the average consumer. For example, a younger population will be more likely to purchase items using new technology.

Culture Values, the ideas or principles you think are important, are influenced by your culture. In turn, your values influence your purchases and the type of advertising message that will appeal to you. If your culture places a high value on family, advertisements that emphasize and reinforce the value of family will connect to your experience. Advertisements that appear to diminish those values may seem insulting or offensive. Because the offensive advertisement doesn't connect to your experience, it won't persuade you to buy anything.

Rituals reinforce your values every time they are performed. For example, sharing family dinners and special events with family members reinforces the value of family. However, rituals are different in every culture, even if the same events are celebrated. Birthdays aren't celebrated with cake, ice cream, and party hats in every culture. If your client makes birthday cakes or party favors, you should understand the birthday rituals of the proposed consumer.

CHECKPOINT

Why is market analysis done?

____

____

THINK CRITICALLY

1. Explain the components of an advertising plan.

2. What is the purpose of an advertising plan?

3. What is the most important factor described in an advertising plan?

4. Why is it important to know why current customers buy a product?

5. What factors must be considered in a global advertising campaign?

MAKE CONNECTIONS

6. **HISTORY** Using the library or Internet, look up the North American Free Trade Agreement (NAFTA). What were the arguments for and against the agreement when it was proposed? How has the agreement worked out so far? What impact has it had on trade? Write your findings in a one-page paper.

7. **SOCIAL STUDIES** Select another country. Using the library or Internet, identify the demographic information for the country. Write a one-page paper describing the country's population.

LESSON 4.2

SET OBJECTIVES AND BUDGET

DETERMINE the objectives of the advertising campaign

EXPLAIN the methods that can be used to set the advertising budget

SELECT CAMPAIGN OBJECTIVES

How do you know if you have succeeded or failed, won or lost? Without goals, you don't know if you have succeeded or not.

Why do advertising campaigns fail? Although there are many reasons an advertising plan might fail, the failure can often be tracked to poor or unreasonable goals for the advertising campaign. Like you, an advertising plan needs clear and reasonable goals to succeed. Without clear goals, an advertising campaign can wander aimlessly without accomplishing anything.

Advertising has two *general* goals.

1. Increase consumer awareness of the company, product, or service.
2. Persuade consumers to try the product or service and return to buy it again.

ON THE $CENE

Raymond Navarro owns several small businesses that rent vacation equipment such as canoes, mountain bicycles, and scuba gear. The rental sites are located in three states. Currently, the name of each rental site is unique. This year he plans to unite the businesses under one name and provide a single phone number that customers can use to reserve equipment at any business location. He collected and saved customer information at each site for insurance purposes. Bright Ideas Advertising Agency is currently developing an advertising plan for him. What objectives should be listed in the plan? What other recommendations would you make?

These general goals are true for almost any business. However, they are not specific enough to help select a target segment and choose a positioning strategy for an advertising campaign. There are several standard *specific* advertising goals. Most businesses would list one or more of the following goals as objectives for advertising campaigns.

1. Increase consumer awareness of the advertiser's brand.
2. Change consumer attitudes about the advertiser's product.
3. Promote replacement of outdated products with new products using superior technology.
4. Persuade the consumer to try a sample of the product.
5. Persuade consumers to buy the advertiser's type of product.
6. Convert a consumer that used the product once into a regular user.
7. Persuade consumers to switch from a competitor's product.
8. Increase sales.

Increase Consumer Awareness As a consumer, you are more likely to purchase a brand that you recognize than an unknown brand. **Top-of-the-mind awareness** identifies the leading brands in a specific product category by asking a consumer to name brands in that category. This is an easy test to conduct. What brands do you think of when someone mentions facial tissues?

Change Consumer Attitudes Negative attitudes toward an advertiser or the advertiser's product affect sales. Additional information or humor might be used to create a better image for the company or product. The advertiser must decide if the reason for the negative attitude should be addressed in the advertising campaign. Doing so has advantages and disadvantages. For example, bringing up the reason could emphasize the fact that the issue was recognized and fixed or could make it sound like a legitimate concern. It is very difficult to change a negative attitude.

New Products Advertisers want to encourage current customers to buy a newer model in the same product line. This type of advertising encourages brand loyalty in expensive or technological products, such as cars or computers.

Samples Persuading consumers to try a sample of the product is a way of getting a foot in the door. When the consumer tries a sample, the product must meet or exceed the advertised benefits. If the consumer is pleased with the sample, a purchase or repeated purchases may follow.

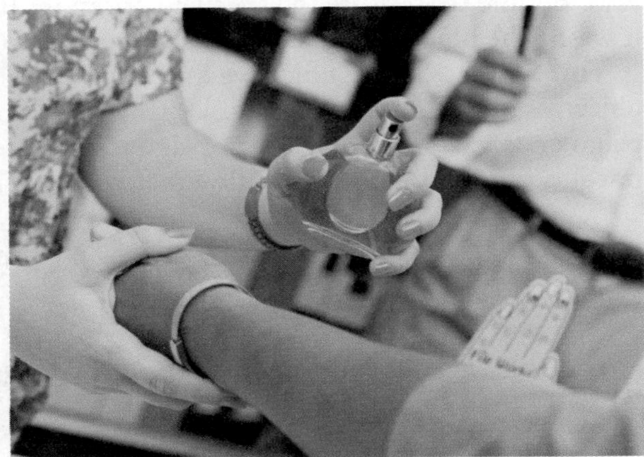

Purchase Intent Persuading consumers to buy the advertiser's product or a similar product increases the size of the

Clip several advertisements from various print media. Can you identify the specific objectives of the advertisements? What information in an advertisement told you the objective? What methods does the advertisement use to reach the objective? Is the advertisement successful?

market. It does not guarantee a larger share of the market for the advertiser, but making the market larger means that both companies in the market will make more sales. The charts below show how this works.

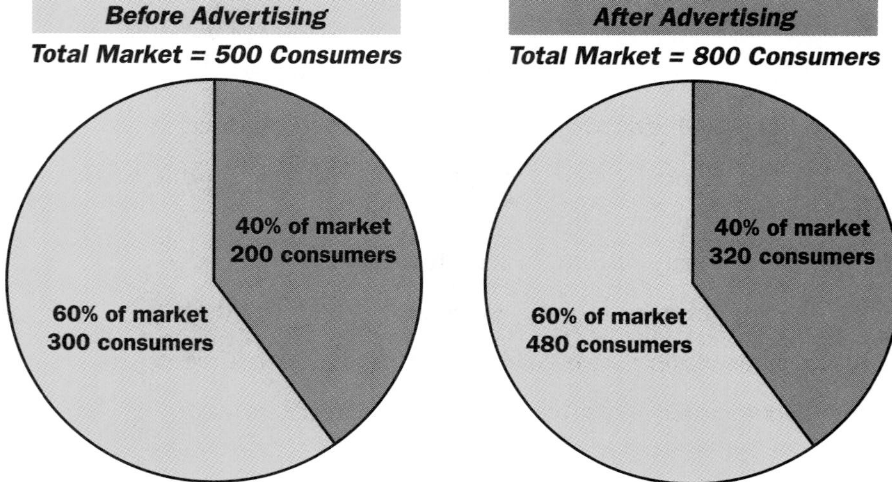

Create a Regular User Trying to convert an occasional user into a regular user is more likely if the user is not brand loyal.

Brand Switching Persuading a consumer who is loyal to another brand to switch brands is one of the most difficult advertising tasks.

Increase Sales The purpose of every campaign is to increase sales. However, this may be done directly or indirectly. A sale is meant to directly increase purchases. An advertisement that improves consumers' attitudes toward a company will indirectly increase sales.

MEASURE SUCCESS

An objective and the conditions for meeting the objective must be clearly stated and include criteria to measure the success of the campaign.

Measure the Result The objective must specify a value that can be measured before and after the advertising campaign. For example, an objective might be to increase brand recognition from 20 percent to 23 percent.

Measurement Methods The objective must specify a method of measuring the result. For example, brand recognition can be measured by surveys. Be sure to measure the specified criterion. It's nice if sales increase, but if it wasn't the objective, it isn't fair to measure it to determine success.

Time Period The objective must specify the time period in which the objective must be accomplished. Usually the time period ends when the campaign ends. So, a three-week campaign to increase brand recognition 5% was not successful if brand recognition increased 5% in the next year.

did you KNOW?

When Apple Computers created the first Macintosh in 1984, customers exhibited an amazing level of brand loyalty. Yet by 1987, 42 percent of Macintosh users were switching to PCs using the Windows operating system. Apple seemed to be eliminated. However, in 1998 the company came back strongly when it introduced the iMac model with an impressive advertising campaign.

Why is brand recognition important to an advertiser?

____

____

SET A BUDGET

Good advertising costs money—money to develop, distribute, and evaluate. Usually the amount to be spent on advertising is determined by the advertiser. Many methods are not very successful.

Affordable Method This is a poor method of setting a budget that is commonly used by small, inexperienced businesses. Basically, the firm spends what it thinks it can afford. It doesn't know if it is spending too much or too little. Only after years of experience can the correct spending level be determined.

Historical Method This is another poor method of setting an advertising budget. The amount for the current budget is based on the amount you were able to afford last year. To calculate the current budget, multiply last year's budget by the rate of inflation. Of course, since the amount you spent last year was determined by what you could afford, this budget is even less reasonable. It's based on what you could afford last year. It does not consider any changes that have happened to your business since last year, such as new competition. Also, since it is based on historical data, a new business can't use this method.

Percentage of Sales Large companies commonly use this method. The amount for the current budget is a percentage of last year's sales or a percentage of the sales you expect to make this year. A higher percentage is commonly spent on new products. It costs more to build a consumer's awareness of a new product. Companies shouldn't spend less than 10 to 12 percent of the expected sales of the new product. Companies might decide to spend a much higher percentage, as much as 35 percent, if they are comfortable with the expected sales.

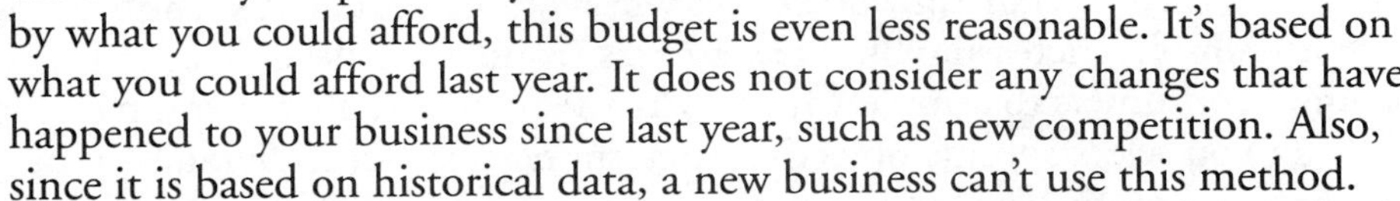

Percentage of sales is a common method of calculating an advertising budget. Air Ticket, a small airline company, wants to calculate an advertising budget for a new commuter route from San Diego to San Francisco. Air Ticket expects to earn $750,000 on the new route and wants to spend 15 percent of the expected sales on the advertising. How much will Air Ticket spend on advertising?

SOLUTION

Advertising budget = Sales × Percentage
Advertising budget = $750,000 × 0.15
Advertising budget = $112,500

Air Ticket's advertising budget is $112,500 for the new route.

This method does have some disadvantages. If sales are decreasing, spending on advertising will also decrease. This could be bad if the business would benefit from an increase in advertising. Also, this method could lead to overspending because the funds have been budgeted for advertising without considering the amount of advertising needed.

Share-of-Voice This method is based on the amount spent by your competition. The idea is to spend more than your competition so that consumers become more aware of your product than your competitor's product. Although many companies use this method, it has some disadvantages. It relies heavily on your competitor's budget decisions.

1. Your competitor's spending information might be impossible to obtain.
2. Your competitor might not be setting a reasonable budget.
3. The same amount of money will not automatically create a campaign of the same quality.
4. Your competitor may have a different objective, requiring a different budget.

Objective and Task This is the only method that uses the relationship between what you want to accomplish and what you want to spend. Because this method uses your objectives, your objectives must be specific and clear. The budget must enable you to achieve your objectives.

Obtaining each level of your objectives will require a different spending level. For example, increasing brand awareness requires one level of spending. Persuading consumers to sample your product requires a higher spending level. After you select specific objectives, determine costs for individual tasks. Costs are based on the level of the task you want to accomplish.

Task	Description
Reach	Geographic and demographic target
Frequency	Number of exposures needed to meet objectives
Time Frame	Timing of exposures over a set period of time
Production	Cost to create advertisements
Media	Cost to buy media time
Ancillary Costs	Related costs not included in any other category
Promotional Costs	Coordination of marketing effort

After the budget is determined, compare the cost to the standard amount for your industry and previous budgets for your company. Finally, set a time frame, evaluate the budget, and make any necessary changes.

What information is used to calculate the budget in the worst method?

____

____

THINK CRITICALLY

1. Why should there be specific objectives in the advertising plan?

2. Why is sampling a good advertising technique?

3. What is one of the most difficult advertising objectives?

4. What is the basis for the share-of-voice method?

5. Why can't a new company use the historical method to determine its advertising budget?

MAKE CONNECTIONS

6. **COMMUNICATION** Write specific objectives for Raymond Navarro's vacation equipment rental business. Be sure to include measurement and time information.

7. **RESEARCH** Contact media providers in your area. Make a chart of the advertising rates. What kind of consumer does each option reach?

LESSON 4.3
COMPLETE THE ADVERTISING PLAN

DESCRIBE the strategy section of an advertising plan

IDENTIFY methods of evaluating the success of an advertising plan

STRATEGY AND EXECUTION

The strategy for a play in a game can be drawn with Xs, Os, and arrows to show the players' movements during the play. The Xs and Os provide a map to tell the players how to perform the strategy.

In an advertising plan, the strategy section describes the plan for the advertising message. The strategy consists of identifying the target segment, selecting a positioning strategy, and choosing the type of advertisement.

IDENTIFY THE TARGET SEGMENT

The target segment is a subgroup of the market that is chosen to be the focus of the marketing and advertising campaign. The target segment is selected because consumers in the segment are those most likely to buy the product or

ON THE $CENE

Bright Ideas Advertising Agency is developing an advertising plan for Raymond Navarro's vacation equipment rental business. After analyzing the customer information he collected, the agency grouped his current customers into two categories. The first category is physically active individuals between the ages of 20 and 35. The second category is families that rent equipment for family vacations. Who should be the target segment? What strategies should be listed in the plan?

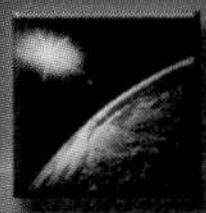

service. There are four strategies for selecting a target market, and the advertiser chooses based on personal philosophy.

1. ***Undifferentiated Marketing*** Businesses produce only one product and sell it to the entire market with a single marketing mix.
2. ***Differentiated Marketing*** Businesses produce many products, each with its own marketing mix, designed to satisfy different segments of the market.
3. ***Concentrated Marketing*** Businesses direct all of the firm's marketing resources toward satisfying a small segment of the total market.
4. ***Micromarketing*** Businesses target potential customers at basic levels, such as zip code, occupation, lifestyle, or individual households.

SELECT A POSITIONING STRATEGY

Positioning is the process of making an advertiser's product different from other products in the consumer's mind. The positioning strategy is used to develop the complete marketing strategy aimed at a target segment. The positioning strategy is designed to achieve a certain attitude in the prospective buyer's mind.

The positioning theme creates a focus for the advertising campaign. *Benefit positioning* selects a single benefit that users might believe is important. *User positioning* emphasizes the consumer's lifestyle, demonstrating how the product fits into that lifestyle. *Competitive positioning* focuses on the differences between your product and other similar products.

CHOOSE THE TYPE OF ADVERTISING

Several types of advertisements are meant to affect the consumer in different ways. Brand advertising highlights the brand name. Informative advertising teaches consumers about product benefits. Comparative and defensive advertising compare two or more products. Persuasive advertising influences consumers by showing happy customers. Select the type of advertising that fits the positioning strategy and objectives.

EXECUTION

Execution is the process of carrying out the strategy. It includes creating the advertisements and placing them in the appropriate media. These important components of advertising are covered in Chapters 5 and 6.

What are the three parts of developing an advertising strategy?

____

____

EVALUATE THE SUCCESS OF THE ADVERTISING PLAN

The final piece of the advertising plan is the evaluation standards that are used to determine the success level of the advertising campaign. The success of the campaign is critical to both the advertiser and the agency. Therefore, it is important that they both understand and agree to the objectives, the measured value that will indicate success, and the measurement tools.

EVALUATE A CAMPAIGN

Why should you evaluate an advertising campaign? Compare the results at the end of an advertising campaign to the objectives in the advertising plan to measure your success. It is also important to calculate your **return on investment**, the amount you earn from the money you spend. Advertising is expensive. The profit you earn because of advertising must justify the amount you spend on advertising.

It is also helpful to determine the individual elements that worked or did not work. This will help you make changes in the future to improve the campaign or use the same elements in a similar campaign.

Difficulties It is challenging to evaluate an advertising campaign. Some results, such as changing a consumer's attitude, are difficult to measure. Measurements may be hard to make because the campaign occurs over an extended period of time. It is difficult to isolate the effects of the campaign. For example, did sales of fans double because of the campaign or because temperatures rose to the high 80s?

HIERARCHY OF CHANGE

Changing an individual's behavior is difficult. There is a hierarchy, or order, of change that can occur. You are more likely to remember information from an advertisement than to change your behavior because of it.

MEASURING SUCCESS FOR ONLINE ADVERTISEMENTS The online version of the *New York Times,* NYTimes.com, provides thorough feedback to its online advertisers. Advertisers receive detailed information about the individuals viewing their advertisements. Consumers fill out a questionnaire when they enter the web site. The answers to the questionnaire are saved with a record of what visitors read, how long they spent on each page, and the type of software they used to access the web site. It's also recorded when consumers click on an advertisement for more information. Advertisers are told where the advertisement was located, so they also learn the best placement for their future advertisements.

THINK CRITICALLY What are the benefits to the advertiser? Are there disadvantages for anyone? If so, what are they?

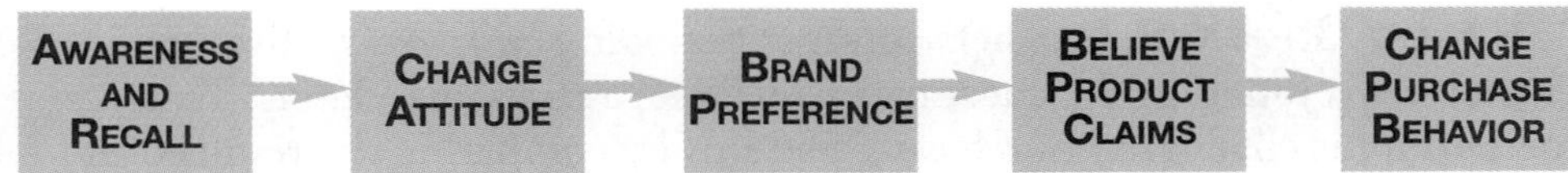

Awareness and Recall Consumers are aware of a brand if they recognize the brand name. Recall includes remembering some product features.

Change Attitude Changing an attitude is a common objective. Having an opinion implies that the consumer is already familiar with the brand.

Brand Preference Preference occurs when a consumer believes that one brand is better than others.

Believe Product Claims This implies that the consumer remembers specific product claims. Conviction occurs when the consumer is ready to take an action, such as make a trial purchase.

Change Purchase Behavior The highest level of change occurs when the consumer's purchasing behavior is modified. This consumer will become a repeat buyer.

MEASUREMENT TOOLS

After an advertising campaign, many tools can be used to measure objectives such as increasing consumer awareness, changing consumer attitude, and persuading consumers to switch to a different brand. Generally if you measure a consumer's knowledge, attitudes, and behavior before the campaign, measuring the same characteristics after the campaign will measure the success of the campaign. This is the most effective method of judging a campaign's impact.

It is important to (1) measure the results of the listed objectives only and (2) use the right measurement tool to evaluate the results. Don't measure a value that was not an objective of the advertising campaign. For example, don't measure consumer attitude if the objective was brand awareness.

Awareness and Recall Testing Several measurement tools rate a consumer's brand awareness and recall. *Unaided recall* asks a consumer to remember the elements of an advertisement without any prompting by the interviewer. This demonstrates the highest recall level. The interviewer might ask "Do you remember any commercials you saw on television last night?" The consumer would then be able to describe a commercial, including the product brand that was advertised.

Aided recall requires prompting by the interviewer. The interviewer might prompt the consumer with the brand name of the advertised product. The consumer could then respond with details about the commercial. However, the information is less set in the consumer's memory.

Coincidental Studies Some measurements can be taken at the same time as the campaign. These **coincidental studies** provide real-time information about the campaign's impact. Telephone surveys are a common tool.

Tracking Studies A series of coincidental studies can be performed over the life of the campaign. These *tracking studies* follow the consumers' reactions over a period of time.

Consumer Diaries Consumer panelists keep a diary of their purchases over a period of time. In the diary, they record the item purchased, the price of the item, and any advertising that might have affected their purchasing decisions. This method works well to measure objectives based on the quantity of sales.

Select a product you know well. Write 15 multiple-choice survey questions to analyze the consumer's knowledge, attitude, or purchasing behavior. Make sure the questions you write don't tell the consumer what answers you want or expect. Ask a partner to evaluate your questions.

Pantry Check Researchers conduct periodic *pantry checks*, listing purchased items found in the consumer panelists' pantries and closets. This method finds changes in purchasing patterns by comparing the results over time. This method also works well to measure any objectives based on the quantity of sales.

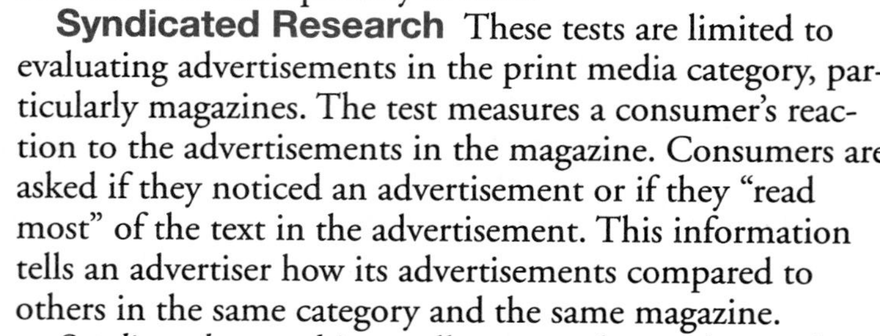

Syndicated Research These tests are limited to evaluating advertisements in the print media category, particularly magazines. The test measures a consumer's reaction to the advertisements in the magazine. Consumers are asked if they noticed an advertisement or if they "read most" of the text in the advertisement. This information tells an advertiser how its advertisements compared to others in the same category and the same magazine.

Syndicated research is usually not used to evaluate advertisements in the broadcast media. Because it is suited more for print media, results aren't reliable when the questions are applied to a different type of media.

Custom Research Techniques A variety of test methods fit into this category. You are probably familiar with one of the most common methods—the *mall intercept method.* Those people at the mall with the clipboards who try to convince you to answer a few questions are probably conducting marketing research. Mall intercept and telephone surveys are popular and cost-effective methods of conducting research.

Consumer panels can be used to collect a variety of feedback. Panel members can list things they like or dislike about the advertisement. Advertisers can verify that the intended message is getting through by asking panelists to identify the most important benefit the product offers.

Mail questionnaires elicit varied levels of feedback. Although they are low cost and simple to conduct, they often have a low response rate. People just don't bother to fill them out and send them in. At one time, some advertisers sent a dollar with the questionnaires. They thought people would be more likely to respond if they were "paid" for their time.

INTERPRETING RESULTS

After all the responses are received, they must be interpreted accurately. The conclusions must be reasonable. Remember that the conclusions will be used to evaluate the advertising campaign and the performance of the advertising agency. Often the agency's payment and the advertiser's future depend on the result of the campaign.

Why do you calculate your return on investment?

____

____

THINK CRITICALLY

1. How is the positioning strategy used in the advertising plan?

2. What is the execution part of the advertising plan?

3. Why should you evaluate an advertising campaign?

4. Explain the first level in the hierarchy of change.

MAKE CONNECTIONS

5. **BUSINESS** Use the library or Internet. Locate more information about the importance of calculating the return on investment. Write a one-page description of how it is calculated and how it is used.

6. **COMMUNICATION** Create a chart of the evaluation methods. Include the type of objective that can be evaluated by each method.

7. **PROBLEM SOLVING** What type of positioning strategy should Bright Ideas Advertising Agency recommend for Raymond Navarro's vacation equipment rental business?

REVIEW

CHAPTER SUMMARY

LESSON 4.1 Develop an Advertising Plan

A. The advertising plan consists of the introduction, situational analysis, objectives, budget, strategy, execution methods, and evaluation. One of the most important strategic purposes of marketing is the image of a brand.

B. The situational analysis examines the conditions that affect the product or service. The situational analysis reviews the company and product history, evaluates the product's strengths and weaknesses, defines the target segment, and evaluates the competition.

LESSON 4.2 Set Objectives and Budget

A. The objectives state the goals of the advertising campaign. Two general goals of advertising are to increase consumer awareness of the company, product, or service and to persuade consumers to try the product or service and return to buy it again.

B. Several methods can be used to set the budget for the advertising campaign—the affordable method, the historical method, the percentage-of-sales method, the share-of-voice method, and the objective and task method. The objective and task method uses the relationship between what you want to accomplish and what you want to spend

LESSON 4.3 Complete the Advertising Plan

A. The strategy section describes the plan for the advertising message and consists of identifying the target segment, selecting a positioning strategy, and choosing the type of advertisement.

B. Methods to evaluate the success of the advertising campaign include awareness and recall testing, coincidental studies, tracking studies, consumer diaries, pantry checks, syndicated research, and custom research techniques.

VOCABULARY BUILDER

Choose the term that best fits the definition. Write the letter of the answer in the space provided. Some terms may not be used.

____ **1.** Examines the customers and their motives for buying the product

____ **2.** Summarizes the most important information needed in order to make decisions concerning the advertising plan

____ **3.** Examines developments and trends in the industry

____ **4.** Identifies the document's structure and the material that will be covered in the advertising plan

____ **5.** Examination of conditions and circumstances that affect the product or service

a. advertising plan
b. coincidental studies
c. competitor analysis
d. executive summary
e. industry analysis
f. market analysis
g. overview
h. positioning
i. return on investment
j. situational analysis
k. top-of-the-mind awareness

REVIEW CONCEPTS

6. What are the components of an advertising plan?

7. What does the marketing strategy do?

8. What functions does the situational analysis perform?

9. Based on economic development, what are the groups of countries?

10. What are the common general goals of advertising?

11. What is the effect of increasing purchase intent?

12. Describe the objective and task budgeting method.

13. What are the levels in the hierarchy of change?

14. What are unaided and aided recall?

15. Why isn't syndicated research used to evaluate advertisements in the broadcast media?

APPLY WHAT YOU LEARNED

16. How does the advertising plan benefit the advertiser?

17. What is the most difficult part of the advertising plan to create? Why?

18. How would you find information for the situational analysis?

19. Describe a situation in which you benefited from a company's advertising.

20. Why would a company use an undifferentiated marketing strategy?

MAKE CONNECTIONS

21. BUSINESS Use the Internet or library. Identify a company that sells products in other countries. Look at the annual report for the company. What information does it include about international trade or advertising?

22. BUSINESS Select a small company in your area. Write a possible objective for an advertising campaign.

23. BUSINESS Describe a recent advertising campaign in your area that included you in the target segment.

24. ECONOMICS Use the library or Internet. What impact has the North American Free Trade Agreement (NAFTA) had on Mexico and Canada?

25. COMMUNICATION Select an advertising campaign that uses a celebrity. Why was that celebrity chosen?

CHAPTER 5

CREATE YOUR ADVERTISEMENT

LESSONS

5.1 SELECT A STRATEGY

5.2 WRITE THE MESSAGE

5.3 PUT THE AD IN PRINT

5.4 PUT THE AD ON TELEVISION

CAREERS IN ADVERTISING

SICOLAMARTIN, INC.

SicolaMartin, Inc., located in Austin, Texas, is one of the top ten marketing and advertising agencies specializing in high-tech business-to-business clients. SicolaMartin helps companies succeed in a rapidly changing environment. They have expertise in the strategic development of corporate, brand, product, and program positioning, messaging, and brand identity systems.

A Senior MarCom (marketing communications) Writer can create and write long copy for high-tech clients, supervise contracted marcom writers, and identify additional freelance marcom writers who perform reliably. This person also maintains a positive business relationship with clients and freelancers.

The position requires a college degree, an interest in technology, and seven years of experience, some of which should be in a high-tech area.

THINK CRITICALLY

1. What about the position of Senior MarCom Writer appeals to you?
2. How much time do you think this person spends writing and how much time is spent supervising other writers?

The Chapter 5 video for this module introduces the concepts in this chapter.

PROJECT

Create Advertisements

PROJECT OBJECTIVES

- Select a message strategy that can be used in different media
- Create an integrated advertising campaign using print and television advertisements

GETTING STARTED

Read through the Project Process below. Make a list of any materials you will need. Decide how you will get the needed materials or information.

- The Running Shoe specializes in shoes for runners. The owner is a long-distance runner who usually finishes in one of the top five positions in local marathon and minimarathon races. She is well known among local runners. The Running Shoe is small but has become very profitable since the owner opened a catalog service five years ago, then branched to Internet sales two years ago.
- Look in newspapers and magazines for advertisements for related fields such as sports equipment and running shoe stores. Bring in the advertisements. Look on the Internet for banner ads relating to sports equipment and running shoes. Bring in printouts of the banner ads you find.

PROJECT PROCESS

Part 1 **LESSON 5.1** Select a message strategy that will be effective for the business. Write a slogan for the business.

Part 2 **LESSON 5.2** Fill in the components of the creative plan by determining the target segment, advertising message, and so on.

Part 3 **LESSON 5.3** Create a print advertisement for a newspaper or magazine using the creative plan.

Part 4 **LESSON 5.4** Create a storyboard for a television commercial that carries the same advertising message.

CHAPTER REVIEW

Project Wrap-up Draw the print advertisement and storyboard for the television commercial. Present them to the class. Be prepared to perform the television commercial.

LESSON 5.1

SELECT A STRATEGY

PREPARE advertising messages driven by the product

PREPARE advertising messages driven by the user

BASE YOUR ADVERTISING MESSAGE ON THE PRODUCT

Advertisers want to capture your attention when you are doing something else. You do not drive down the street, flip through a magazine, or watch television hoping to see an advertisement. You are there for some other reason. You are trying to get somewhere, read an interesting article, or watch a television program.

Advertisers have only seconds to distract you from your main purpose. Once an advertisement has distracted you, it must keep your attention and deliver a message. This **message strategy**, the advertiser's objectives and the methods used to carry out the objectives, is a key component of the advertising plan. Objectives are based on attributes of the product or the user.

ON THE $CENE

Ling Jen owns a chain of 50 jewelry stores throughout the United States. She has come to your agency because she wants to launch an advertising campaign that uses several types of media. She is interested in print, radio, and television advertisements. Right now, she has to decide what type of message strategy she should use. The jewelry is high quality. There are also a small number of custom design orders every year. What type of message strategy would you recommend? What specific message would you create?

BRAND RECALL

Advertisers want to be the first brand you remember when you think of a product. If they are not first, they want to be among the first few brands you remember. The **evoked set** is a short list of brand names you think of when a product or service is mentioned. Once a brand name is in a consumer's evoked set, it is then possible for the brand name to become a consumer's preferred brand. The next step most advertisers hope to achieve is for the consumer to become loyal to the brand.

Repetition One of the easiest methods of getting you to remember a brand name is *repetition*. The more you hear the brand name, the more likely you are to remember it. Repetition includes the frequency of encountering the advertisement and the frequency of the brand name in the advertisement.

Slogans and Jingles A catchphrase meant to help you remember a brand name is a **slogan**. A slogan is memorable because of characteristics such as simplicity, rhyme, and rhythm. A jingle has the same characteristics and purpose, but it is set to music.

How many slogans and jingles can you remember? Make a list. Can you match those phrases to the associated product? How many of the products do you buy?

BRAND PREFERENCE

Advertisers want you to like their brand. Liking puts a product closer to brand preference. If you dislike a brand, it will never become your preferred brand, even if it is in your evoked set. Like and dislike are feelings about a product that can be affected by advertisements.

Feel Good Advertisements that make you feel good anticipate that you will transfer that good feeling to the product. You prefer to do business with companies that make you feel good and companies that you like. This method does not always work. You can like an advertisement without liking the product or the company.

Humor Using humor in an advertisement can be risky. The humor has to tie directly to the product, or consumers will remember the joke but not the brand name or product. Humorous messages wear out quickly. After you have heard the joke a few times, it just does not seem as funny.

KEY ATTRIBUTE

Linking the brand name to a single characteristic encourages you to remember the brand name and the attribute. Usually trying to link a brand name to several attributes is not very successful. A short and simple advertising message is more likely to be remembered.

Unique Selling Proposition Advertisements that emphasize only a single key attribute use the *unique selling proposition* philosophy. The brand name will help you remember the attribute, and the attribute will help you remember the brand name.

SOCIAL CONTEXT

All objects have some meaning or value in society. Advertisers believe they can give their products value in society by the social setting in the advertisement.

Slice of Life These advertisements select a moment in time when the product is being used. The social setting around the product gives it meaning. For example, an older wealthy couple dancing on the deck of a cruise ship could suggest that the cruise is a reward for living well.

Light Fantasy These advertisements encourage consumers to picture themselves as wealthy, athletic, or lucky. The brand becomes associated with the desired characteristic in the advertisement.

BRAND IMAGE

The brand's image is the characteristic that most consumers associate with the brand. Brand image is very important to a company's long-term success.

Image Advertisements that create an image for a brand name are usually placed in visual media such as television, print, or the Internet. Image advertisements do not give information about the brand. They usually rely on the picture rather than the words to create the image.

What is the purpose of a slogan or jingle?

____

____

BASE YOUR ADVERTISING MESSAGE ON THE CONSUMER

Advertising strategy can also be based on the impact on the consumer. These strategies often make emotional appeals or ask the consumer to make or change some type of action or behavior.

FEAR

Fear can be a powerful motivator. It can be used to motivate consumers to take some action, such as buying or using the advertised product to protect them from danger. This type of advertisement informs you of the risks associated with not using the brand. Products such as security systems, smoke detectors, and insurance are good candidates for this type of strategy. The products will protect you from the dangers depicted in the advertisement. This strategy is not always successful. Consumers may focus on the fear rather than the product that will protect them from the danger. They may even develop a negative attitude toward the advertiser for telling them about the danger.

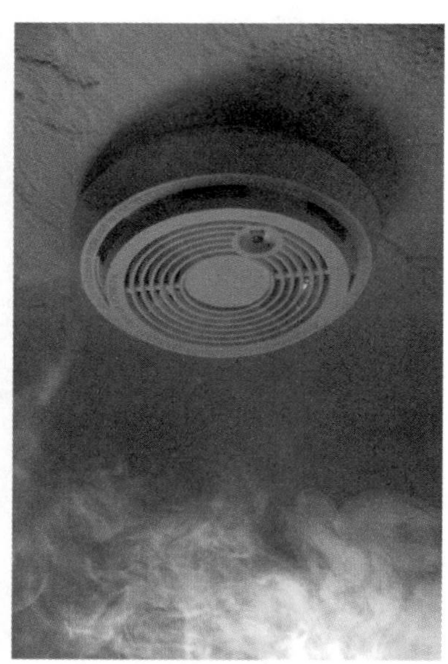

ANXIETY

Anxiety is not as powerful as fear. It is concern about something rather than fear of it. Consumers often will buy a product that will protect them from an anxious situation. Like the fear strategy, this type of advertisement informs you of the risks associated with not using the brand. When advertisers use the anxiety strategy, they must show you the danger and present a product that will prevent or help you avoid the danger. Personal products such as mouthwash and shampoo are good candidates for this type of strategy. These products will protect you from embarrassing social situations.

These advertisements often portray the consumer in a situation that would normally create anxiety and present the solution to the anxiety. A common situation might involve a job interview. Although there are many aspects of the situation that can produce anxiety, you can use the advertised brand of breath mints to protect you from not getting the job because of bad breath.

TRANSFORM CONSUMER'S EXPERIENCE

Every experience you have consists of more than the actions that occurred. For example, a trip to an amusement park with friends is more than a list of the rides you took and the activities you did. It includes the feel of the sun on your face, the splash of the cold water from the log flume, and the pleasure of laughing with your friends over silly jokes or observations. How can you pack all of that into an advertising strategy?

Your experience as a consumer can be transformed to enhance the experience. If the transformational strategy is effective, the emotions and memories suggested in the advertisement will be triggered every time you view the advertisement and buy or use the product. For example, every time you drink a specific brand of flavored coffee, you might remember lingering over coffee, chatting with friends, or relaxing at the end of a hectic day. Those emotions and memories will be linked to buying and drinking the coffee brand, enhancing the experience, and reinforcing your behavior.

DIRECT RESPONSE

The direct response strategy encourages consumers to act immediately. It communicates a sense of urgency to buying the product. The expected response is personal contact initiated by the consumer. The direct response also provides immediate feedback for the advertiser.

Call Now The direct response strategy is becoming more common. It often includes some type of price-based reward for contacting the advertiser immediately. Many situations are ideal for the direct response strategy.

GENERIC BRANDS There are generic equivalents for most products, including computers and computer parts. The difference between generic and proprietary parts is that generic parts are made to meet general specifications. Generic parts work for most computer systems, but they are not guaranteed to work in any specific system. Proprietary parts are manufactured for a specific system and are guaranteed to work in that system. Because generic parts are manufactured in bulk, they are significantly less expensive than proprietary parts.

THINK CRITICALLY Why would a consumer buy a generic brand? What are the benefits of buying a proprietary brand? Which would you prefer to buy? Why? Have you ever used a generic product? Have you ever seen one advertised?

Mail-order companies often send coupons to customers for orders placed within a certain time period. Television commercials offer discounts or additional merchandise for the next 20 callers. Internet advertisements promise special benefits if you click on the banner advertisement.

PERSUASION

The goal of the persuasive strategy is to convince consumers that a specific brand is better. Persuasion requires more work by the advertiser and the consumer. Persuading consumers is more difficult than using the fear strategy. The message is more complicated in a persuasive advertisement. Most persuasive strategies require some thought by the consumer to understand the message. There are many methods of persuasion.

Reason-Why Advertisers can use reason and logic to persuade the consumer. They present reasons why the brand is superior, for example, by listing attributes of the product. Attributes for buying an automobile might include legroom, gas efficiency, and price. There are two rules to follow. First, the reasons must make sense to the consumer. Second, the reasons must be important to the consumer. An advertiser can choose any attributes of the product that follow these rules. Attributes not important to consumers would not persuade anyone to buy the product. For example, advertising that Brand X cars come in shades of red, blue, and green would not persuade consumers to buy that brand. Gas efficiency and price attract consumers who are economical, while additional legroom might attract tall consumers or those interested in comfort.

Hard-Sell The hard-sell strategy creates a sense of urgency in the consumer. The urgency is usually created by a time limit. There are many examples of this strategy. A furniture store might advertise an annual sale that will end Wednesday. Consumers have become accustomed to this type of advertisement, making this strategy less effective.

Comparison Advertisements that use the comparison strategy can provide a great deal of information, including product attributes and benefits, to consumers. Generally an advertiser compares the brand product to another leading brand that competes for the same target segment. Advertisers have used comparison advertising to sell paper towels and dish detergent, as well as cars, telephone service, and financial products.

Comparisons can be made directly or indirectly. *Direct comparisons* provide a toe-to-toe confrontation by naming the other leading brand. *Indirect comparisons* do not name the competing brand. Performed correctly, the comparison strategy can be very effective.

Effective	Ineffective
Direct comparisons to a brand with more market share	Direct comparisons to a brand with less market share
Indirect comparisons by a brand with moderate market share to brands with more or less market share	Brand is new in the product type
Target segment must not be loyal to a brand	Differences between the brands are insignificant

Testimonial A spokesperson endorsing a product in an advertisement is a testimonial. There are three types of spokespeople.

Celebrity testimonials are given by popular celebrities, including athletes, actors, and models. They are individuals the consumer might want to imitate. The product does not have to be in the celebrity's area of expertise. Athletes recommend athletic shoes and golf clubs, but they also recommend coffee makers and investment firms.

People with recognized experience in a specific field give *expert testimonials*. Doctors recommend over-the-counter medicines for common medical problems. Master chefs recommend kitchen appliances. Several years ago, in a slight twist to this approach, burglars recommended home security systems and antitheft devices.

An average person who uses a product provides the *average-user testimonial*. This user has no expertise or fame and is just like anyone in the target segment. If the product works well for an average person, it should work for anyone. Average users can recommend almost any product—from trucks to athlete's foot remedies.

Demonstration "Show them. Don't tell them." This old saying is a good principle to follow for visual media such as print and television. "Before" and "after" photographs are used to advertise more than diet products. Vinyl siding, lawn care products, and cleaning services can use the demonstration strategy effectively.

Advertorial Limited to print media, the *advertorial* is a special advertising section in a publication. It is designed to look like an editorial placed in the magazine or newspaper. This type of presentation enables the advertiser to provide more information than an advertisement would normally contain. It also lends credibility because it looks like an editorial, news story, or article, rather than an advertisement.

Infomercial An advertiser buys television airtime to broadcast an advertisement called an *infomercial*. Infomercials are usually 30 minutes long, but can last from 5 to 60 minutes. The infomercial is often presented as a documentary. Hosted by a narrator, the program contains demonstrations and testimonials. Infomercials are usually broadcast during off-peak hours, late at night, or during the day on weekends. A product or service can benefit from this approach if the target segment will be watching at that time.

CHECKPOINT

Why is the persuasive strategy difficult?

___

___

THINK CRITICALLY

1. Where is the message strategy described for the advertiser and the agency?

2. Why is a brand's image important?

3. Why isn't the fear strategy always effective?

4. Which strategy provides immediate feedback to the advertiser? Explain.

5. What is the difference between direct and indirect comparisons?

MAKE CONNECTIONS

6. **COMMUNICATION** Look at several advertisements in a magazine. Identify the advertising strategy used in each one. Write a one-page summary describing the clues that helped you identify the strategy.

7. **RESEARCH** Identify two brands in an advertisement using the comparison strategy. Using the library or Internet, look up the companies. Compare the history, product lines, and revenues of the companies. Prepare a report about your findings.

8. **BUSINESS** Select a product that is a current trend. What advertising strategy has the company used? Would you recommend a different strategy? Explain your recommendation.

LESSON 5.2

WRITE THE MESSAGE

EXPLAIN the principles of copywriting

APPLY the principles of copywriting to other media

PRINCIPLES OF COPYWRITING

If someone tells you he is a writer, what do you think he does? You may picture him tapping away on a computer to create a best-selling fiction novel. But there are many kinds of writers. Authors of fiction and nonfiction books, authors of children's books, journalists, technical writers, speech writers, screenplay writers, and advertising copywriters are only a small part of the list of possible careers for writers. To succeed, a writer must learn the guidelines for writing well for the specific career field.

THE CREATIVE PLAN

Good advertisements come from good planning, good ideas, and good copywriting. Like most business activities, it helps to have a plan. The **creative plan** is a guideline to creating and constructing the advertising message. The creative plan coordinates the copywriting, art, and media. The creative plan should have the following elements.

ON THE $CENE

Ling Jen has hired your agency to launch an advertising campaign that uses several types of media, including print, radio, and television advertisements. She has selected the message strategy she should use. What information would affect the creative plan for her business? What features and benefits are associated with her product and her custom design service? Could you write a slogan that is appropriate for her jewelry business?

In a small group, choose a single product. List the features and benefits. What is the primary benefit? How would you emphasize this benefit in an advertisement? Would this benefit appeal to the product's target segment?

Target Segment What market segment has been selected as consumers of this product or service? The intended audience determines the elements you will use to make a connection with them. Remember, if they can't connect to the advertisement, the message will be ignored or rejected.

Advertising Message What do you want the advertisement to accomplish? Do you want consumers to perform some action such as remembering the brand name or linking the brand to a key attribute?

Features and Benefits What are the characteristics of the product, and how do they benefit the target segment? A characteristic that is part of a product or service is a **feature**. A **benefit** is the advantage the consumer gets from that feature. Features are valuable, but it is the benefit that will sell the product. Identify the main benefit of buying or using the product. If you have enough space, you can mention additional benefits, but do not detract from your product's main benefit.

Feature	Benefit
Coffeemaker has an automatic timer	Saves time for you
No-more-tears formula	Won't hurt your eyes
Nonstick surface	Easier to clean

Media How will the message be distributed? It is vital to select the right media to distribute your message, within your budget. Does the product need to be demonstrated or displayed? Television is your best choice. Do not use radio.

Time How long will the advertisement be distributed? Remember, some strategies, such as humor, lose the audience's interest after several viewings.

Mood What is the mood or tone the advertisement should project? The mood should match the message strategy and the product. If you use the fear strategy, the advertisement will be darker. If you are selling engagement rings, the mood should be light, happy, or romantic.

Production Budget How much money can you spend? It all comes down to money. No matter how good the concept is, if the advertiser cannot pay for the advertisement, it will not be produced and distributed.

RESEARCH FIRST

Before you write a single word, do your research. Find out everything possible about the product, the company, and the competition. Take notes, and write down ideas as you research. Do not depend on memory for an important fact or possible idea. You won't use all the information you find, but you do not know which piece of information will be important.

Study the Product Read all the product information you can find. Has the company conducted market research or produced brochures? Are there manuals, installation instructions, or technical descriptions of the product? What does it do? How is it used? What are the features and benefits?

After you have read the literature, interview people at the company. Engineers who designed the product will have a different viewpoint from technicians who install or service the product. Individuals who interact with

customers can provide a different angle. What do customers like most or least about the product? This research can keep you from making a big mistake by selecting the worst feature to highlight in your advertisement.

Study the Company Read the company literature, including brochures, newsletters, and annual reports. Investigate the company's history and its plans for the future. Investigate the company's industry. Is the industry telecommunications, pharmaceuticals, clothing, or something else? Is the industry showing growth? What is the company's image with consumers?

Study the Competition Finally, check out the competition. Go through magazines and newspapers. Clip out every advertisement placed by a competitor. What kind of claims does the competition make? Have they said anything about your company or product? What features and benefits do they stress in their advertisements? Do you have a feature they do not have? If it is of benefit to the consumer, it might become a product focus.

did you KNOW?

A large amount of information about a company, its products, and its competition is available on the Internet. Many companies' web sites also have a copy of their most recent annual report that you can read or download.

ELEMENTS OF GOOD ADVERTISING COPY

Although the basic elements here refer to the print media, many of these same elements are used in broadcast media, billboards, and Internet advertising. The presentation may differ, but the elements are the same. Not every advertisement will use all five elements. In fact, advertisements do not have to contain all the elements to be effective. Use what you need to create the perfect advertising message.

Headline The leading sentence or sentences are usually placed at the top or bottom of the advertisement. The *headline* is intended to attract attention and pull in the reader. This makes the headline the most important element in the advertisement and the most important part of the message.

Headlines can use a positive or negative approach. The positive approach tells consumers what they will gain from buying or using the product. It can do this by highlighting a key benefit. The negative approach tells consumers about the bad things they can avoid by using or buying the product. This approach can also highlight the key benefit.

Headlines should be one of the most important persuasive elements in the advertisement, emphasize the key benefit, have as much information as possible, be brief, include the brand name, and use simple words familiar to the consumer.

Subhead Many advertisements use subheads with the major headline. A *subhead* is a few words, a phrase, or a sentence that is usually placed above or below the headline. The subhead has four important functions. It provides more information about the headline, provides more information about the key benefit, provides information about special offers or opportunities, and lures the consumer into reading the body of the advertisement.

The placement of subheads is not limited to being near the headline. Subheads can also be used in the body if the body copy is long. The subheads guide and direct the consumer through the body text.

Body The main textual element is the *body copy.* Most consumers have already abandoned the advertisement before they get to the body copy. That does not mean that the body is not important. The consumers who read the body copy are the ones most likely to buy your product. Keep the body copy interesting, and make sure it follows the message strategy and tone.

Caption or Call Out If you use photographs or illustrations, the *caption* is another opportunity to deliver your advertising message. *Call outs* are short excerpts from the body copy or provide more information about the art. Consumers will read captions and call outs before they read the body. If the art, rather than the headline, drew the consumer's interest, the caption or call out might be the first thing the consumer reads.

Tag Line The slogan, also called a *tag line,* is a short phrase that is almost a textual logo. It helps to establish an image or a position and increase recall for the brand. The tag line puts your position in simple, friendly terms. The slogan is very important in radio advertising, when a logo cannot be seen.

TIPS TO AVOID COMMON MISTAKES

No matter how good your concept is, you can ruin good copy by making mistakes that distract the consumer from your message. There are several mistakes you can prevent by following these guidelines.

1. Do not get carried away with a clever idea. Make sure all of the text helps to deliver the message. If it does not, delete it.
2. Do not be vague. Be as specific as possible. Stating the number of seconds it takes for a car to go from 0–60 miles per hour is better than saying it is fast.
3. Do not be too wordy. You have limited space to deliver your message. Consumers will lose interest if the advertisement is too long.
4. Do not use clichés or superlatives. Consumers will lose interest, and your product will seem boring or unreliable.
5. Your positioning should be unique, making you different from your competition. If the same advertisement would work for your competitor, it is not a good advertising message.
6. Use language appropriate for your target segment. Consumers will respond better to familiar language patterns.
7. Use humor cautiously. It can be misinterpreted.
8. Concentrate on the strengths of your product rather than criticizing your competition.

Why is the headline important?

____

____

WRITE COPY FOR EACH MEDIA

Each media form presents different challenges for copywriters. For example, you cannot create an effective radio or television advertisement by simply broadcasting the copy you wrote for placement in a magazine. Regardless of the media, it is important to apply the principles of copywriting.

RADIO

Radio is a creative challenge because the medium is sound only. Copywriters must create images in the consumer's mind. Also, except for talk radio, few people actively listen to the radio. It is often just background noise.

Length Most radio spots are 30 or 60 seconds long. This does not seem like much time, but if you time some radio advertisements you will see that quite a lot can be said in 30 seconds.

Format There are four formats for radio advertisements, which provide the structure for writing the radio advertisement.

The *music format* consists of songs and jingles. The music for the song can be written specifically for the advertisement, or it can be an existing song. The music you select should appeal to your target segment. Music can also be played in the background.

The *dialogue format* uses conversation. To avoid sounding like a boring discussion, copywriters use humor to keep the consumer interested.

In the *announcement format,* an announcer, usually the disc jockey or newscaster, reads the product information. If the ad is recorded ahead of time, sound effects and music can be added before it is broadcast.

In the *celebrity announcer format,* a celebrity can act as the announcer to increase consumer interest in the advertisement. A recognizable celebrity voice and a dramatic delivery style increase consumers' attention.

Guidelines The general guidelines for writing good copy apply to radio advertisements, but there are additional tips that are specific to radio. For example, you should use words, sounds, and music to stimulate the consumer's imagination and create images. Repeat the name of the product and the information for contacting the company or buying the product. Emphasize the key benefit. Modify the message for the time, place, and audience. Do not forget to include your slogan at the end of every radio advertisement.

TELEVISION

Radio and television advertising are similar in some ways. However, television adds the magic of moving pictures. Rather than asking the consumer to imagine an product, you can show the product in living color.

Length Like radio, most television spots are 30 or 60 seconds long. Shorter spots, a result of the high cost of the television medium, are occasionally shown. Infomercials run much longer.

Format The additional capabilities of the television medium provide the opportunity to use a variety of formats. One or more will surely fit your advertising message. If they do not fit, you can create a new format that will fit.

Select a commercial for a familiar product, such as toothpaste or clothing. Identify the format and the message strategy. How would you create a magazine advertisement from the commercial? Draw the advertisement, and explain it to the class.

The *demonstration format* is ideal to demonstrate the benefits of your product. The *problem-and-solution format* shows how a difficult situation is eased by the brand. With the *music-and-song format,* the music is the message. The music provides the mood, while the images show the brand.

The *spokesperson format* relies heavily on the text. The visuals merely support the copy. The *dialogue format* also relies heavily on the text, but it involves more characters. The *vignette format* is a series of commercials that feature the same product and characters. Each commercial is similar to a chapter in a book, telling a part of the story. The *narrative format* also tells a story, but not in a series. The mood of these ads is personal and emotional.

Guidelines Make the audio and visual elements work together. Support the video without describing the action. Coordinate the audio and visual elements. Don't just entertain the viewers. Sell the product. Do not lose the purpose of the message by getting caught up in a clever idea. Write flexible copy that will work well in different time lengths. Don't be too wordy. Too much text will interfere with the visuals and overload the consumer. Be consistent with the brand image.

INTERNET

Advertisers and agencies push the envelope a little further every day as the technology develops. Most major companies maintain web sites to provide information about the business or its products. Many companies also sell products from their web sites. Like a store made of brick and mortar, you have to advertise to attract consumers to your site.

Length In size, advertisements are limited to the size of your screen. The length of time the advertisement is available to consumers depends on the web site where the advertisement is displayed.

Format The most exciting feature about Internet advertising is its interactive nature. In most Internet advertising formats, the consumer is in control of the contact, clicking to view more or clicking to leave.

Advertisers can send e-mail directly to the consumer's virtual mailbox. This has upset a large number of Internet users. As a result, most companies do not use this format unless the consumer asks to receive the ads by e-mail.

A paid placement on a web site is a **banner ad**. Consumers interested by the advertisement can click on the banner ad to visit the company's web site or view more information about the product. Most banner ads are only a few inches wide and an inch or two tall.

A *pop-up* advertisement is automatically displayed in a separate window when the user visits a web site. Its size is limited only by the size of the screen.

Guidelines You should keep advertisements simple. Consumers complain if the web page is slow to load because the ads contain a lot of graphics. Also, make sure to provide a link for more information.

CHECKPOINT

Why is radio a creative challenge?

____

____

THINK CRITICALLY

1. What is the difference between a feature and a benefit?

2. How important is production budget in the creative plan?

3. What are the five elements of good advertising copy?

4. What is the most exciting feature about advertising on the Internet?

5. Suppose you work for an advertising agency. A new sandwich shop is opening near the university in your town. Describe and explain the advertising media and format you would recommend.

MAKE CONNECTIONS

6. BUSINESS Investigate an Internet site that displays advertisements. How much traffic does the site have? How are advertising rates set? Describe your findings in a one-page summary.
7. COMMUNICATION Select two formats for the same media or different media. Compare and contrast the characteristics of the formats. How would you distribute the same message in each format?

LESSON 5.3

PUT THE AD IN PRINT

DEVELOP an effective layout for a print advertisement

DESCRIBE the production process for a print advertisement

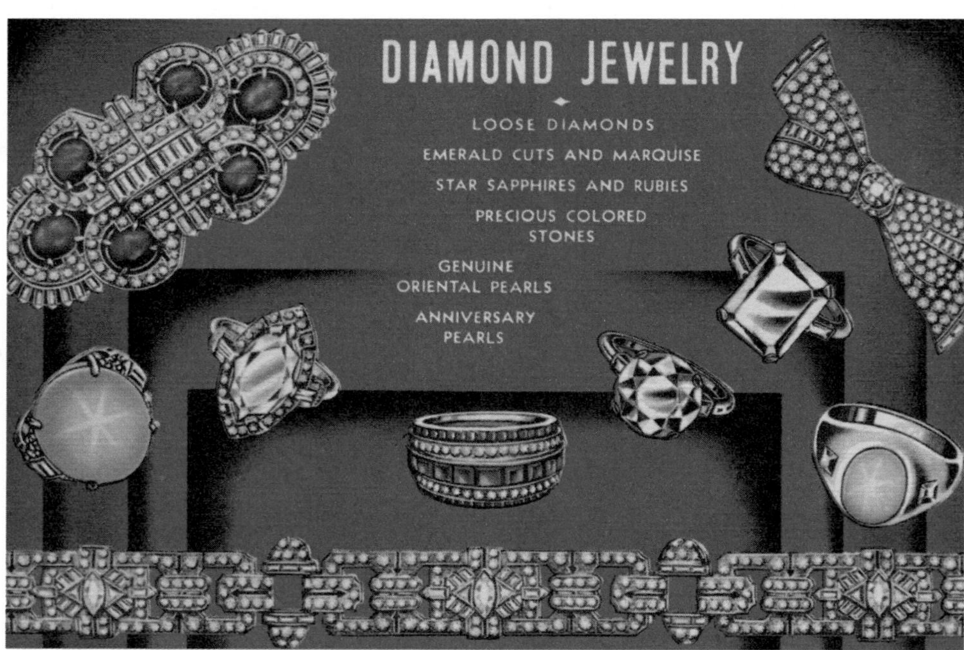

DEVELOP AN EFFECTIVE LAYOUT

What is it about a print advertisement that catches and keeps your attention even though you are in the middle of doing something else? The pictures do not move. There is no catchy tune you can whistle. What is it?

As important as words are to a print advertisement, the element that first catches your eye is usually not words alone. The complete print advertisement consists of words and illustrations arranged in a way to catch your attention and deliver an advertising message.

The copy and the art must work together and follow the creative plan. Generally the copy contains the message. The visual element supports and helps to deliver the message. When referring to advertising, art is the visual element. **Art** is everything in the advertisement that is not copy, including the illustration and design.

ON THE $CENE

Ling Jen has selected the message strategy she should use. Your agency is ready to design the print advertisement. What information in the creative plan will help you design the advertisement? What feature or benefit associated with her product and her custom design service will be the focus?

ILLUSTRATION

The picture in an ad is the *illustration.* It can be any format, including a drawing, painting, photograph, or computer-generated graphic. An illustration is a key part of delivering the advertising message and has several purposes.

- ***Attracts attention.*** The illustration should attract and hold the attention of the target segment. A photograph of an elderly couple dancing on a cruise ship will attract attention from consumers in the same age group. It will probably be completely ignored by a sixteen-year-old.
- ***Makes the brand look heroic.*** Like a stage actor highlighted by a spotlight, the product should be the visual focus of the illustration. This makes the brand look heroic and important.
- ***Tells you about one or more of the features or benefits.*** Photographs from before and after use of the product can be effective.
- ***Creates a mood or an image of the product.*** A bride dancing with her father at her wedding reception produces emotional appeal.
- ***Creates interest in reading the copy.*** Curiosity and interest created by the illustration encourage viewers to become readers.
- ***Creates a social context for the brand.*** This may be one of the most important functions of the illustration. The context links the product to a lifestyle and a target segment.

Components The size, color, and medium (drawing, photograph or graphic) are artistic decisions, but they must follow the creative plan.

- ***Size*** The size of the illustration can determine if a viewer will notice it. The size won't determine if the illustration will help deliver the message.
- ***Color*** Color can be used to highlight the product or its features. Color may be necessary. An ad for paint wouldn't be the same without color. However, color is not always available. Many newspaper ads are black and white.
- ***Medium*** The medium helps to create the mood. A photograph is more "real" because it is a picture of something that exists. A computer graphic is easier to manipulate but may seem less real.

ADVERTISING GLOBALLY

The use of color is important to an advertisement. Colors create moods or emotions. Blue is peaceful and tranquil. Yellow is busy and happy. Red transmits excitement. Colors are also associated with events. Brides wear white to show joy and purity. Funeral attendees wear black to show mourning or grief. However, colors have different meanings in different cultures. In Korea, funeral attendees wear white. In China, brides often wear red.

THINK CRITICALLY What colors do you associate with specific events?

How does an illustration provide social context? How would an illustration attract you as the advertisement's target segment?

DESIGN THE ADVERTISEMENT

Talent and skill are important in creating a good design. The **design** is the arrangement of elements in the advertisement. Artistic talent will create an advertisement that attracts the reader. Skill will ensure that the placement, characteristics, and use of the copy and art components follow the creative plan and deliver the message. There is not a right or wrong design for an ad. There are many elements you can be aware of and manipulate. As you design your ad, keep the principles of order and white space in mind.

Order Your eyes move from left to right when you read. Your eyes naturally follow the same pattern when you look at any other object. Your gaze will normally move from left to right, top to bottom, large objects to small objects, light to dark, and color to no color. Keep this order in mind when you evaluate your design. What is your eye drawn to first? What is the focus of your ad?

White Space The part of your advertisement that has nothing in it is the *white space.* The white space is just as important as anything else in the advertisement. Too little white space makes an advertisement look cluttered and the product look cheap. White space used correctly can draw attention to the most important element and create a dramatic statement.

LAYOUT FOR THE ADVERTISEMENT

The **layout** is a drawing that shows where each element in the advertisement will be placed. There are several stages to creating the layout.

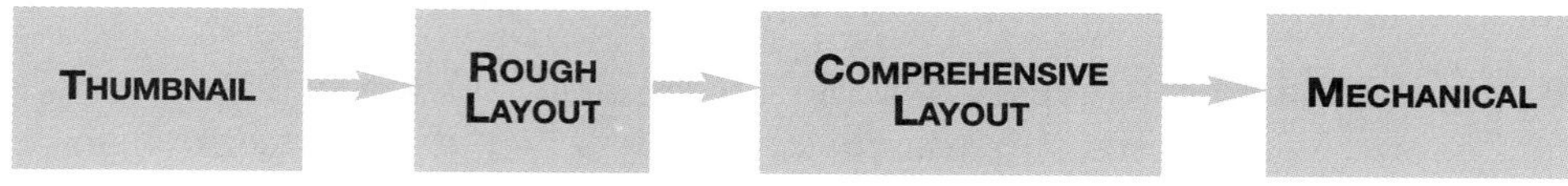

A *thumbnail* is one of the first few drafts of an advertisement. It shows a general idea of where the items will be placed in the final advertisement. It is one-fourth the size of the proposed advertisement.

A *rough layout* is more accurate. It is usually created on the computer so the size of the copy can be determined and placed accurately. It is the size of the proposed advertisement.

A *comprehensive layout* is a polished copy. All the elements are scanned into the computer so everything can be placed accurately. It is printed on a high-quality color printer.

A *mechanical* is the final version. Fine changes are made if necessary, and the advertiser's approval is given. The computer file is ready for production.

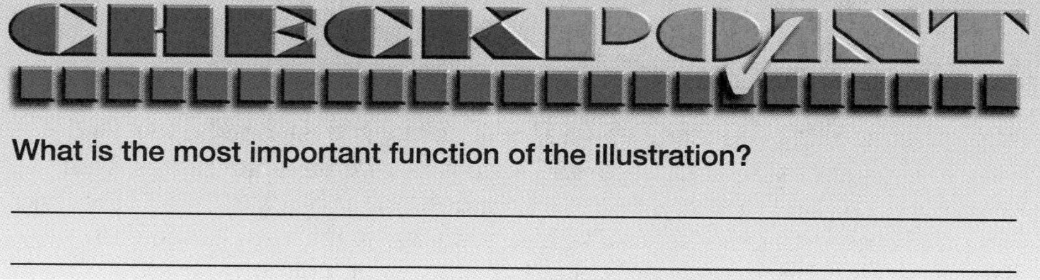

What is the most important function of the illustration?

PRODUCTION OF A PRINT ADVERTISEMENT

The computer has completely revolutionized the print production process. Today the electronic files created by the advertising agency or department are the same files used in the production process. Before the files go to the printer, you know the final advertisement will look as good as you expect.

BEFORE DESKTOP PUBLISHING

Not long ago, printing was a long process with a lot of manual steps. Each letter was loaded separately into a tray to form the words, sentences, and paragraphs. The trays were loaded into the press. Ink was rolled over the type, and it was pressed to the paper. Graphics were even more complicated.

AFTER DESKTOP PUBLISHING

Desktop publishing arrived in the late 1980s. The desktop publishing revolution was driven by leaps in technology and dropping prices in computers. Page layout software made it easy to manipulate text and graphics. Advances in printers enabled you to print your advertisement as it looked on the computer screen.

Proofing Methods Even if you know what to expect, proofing is always a good idea. There's always the chance that some glaring error made it through to this stage. An incorrect date or a misspelled brand name would require an expensive reprint. After viewing the proof, you can make corrections on the computer before the advertisement is printed.

SELECT A PRINT METHOD

If your advertisement will be printed in a publication such as a magazine or newspaper, you do not select a print method. Paper, print quality, and print method will be determined by the publication.

If you are printing the advertisement as a separate direct mail piece or some type of specialty advertising, you will need to make your own decisions about printing methods. There are several factors to consider.

- ***Medium*** Is this a direct mail piece? Is it a special insert, coupon book, or sales flyer?
- ***Amount*** How many are you printing? You might choose a different method if you want 5,000 versus 500,000 copies.
- ***Paper*** Is your advertisement a direct mail piece? Do you plan to use color ink? Is this a glossy sale circular?
- ***Quality*** How important is the piece? Is it meant to last awhile, or is it an inexpensive throwaway piece?
- ***Budget*** How much money do you plan to spend on the finished product?

Consider your answers to these questions before you choose a print production method. Consult your advertising plan.

Offset Lithography This is the most common printing method used. A flat "plate" treated with chemicals is wrapped around a cylinder that attracts ink to printed areas and repels ink from others. The inked image is transferred to a rubber pad on a roller. The roller puts the image on paper.

Lithography, which means "stone writing," was invented in 1798 by a playwright living in Germany. Aloys Senefelder drew a picture with a greasy crayonlike stick on a smooth slab of limestone. When he rolled water and then ink over the picture, the water was repelled by the greasy crayon and clung to the limestone. The reverse occurred with the ink. Senefelder placed a piece of paper against the limestone to transfer the ink to create the image.

Flexography Flexography is similar to offset lithography. However, flexography uses water-based ink. Printing can be done on any surface. This makes it ideal for printing anything from boxes to product labels.

Letterpress This print production process was named because the letters are inked and pressed against the paper, like a rubber stamp. This process has been the main production method for almost five centuries, since Gutenberg invented movable type around 1445. Today letterpress is used in less than 5 percent of print jobs. It is used for embossing, scoring, foil stamping, and die cutting.

Flexography and letterpress are methods of *relief printing*, the process of printing from a raised surface. Relief printing is the oldest printing technique. The Chinese used it as long ago as 200 A.D. The oldest known book was printed in China around 860 A.D. using carved wooden blocks.

Gravure In the fourteenth century, artists began using methods of gravure. Gravure prints from an engraved copper plate. This method is commonly used to print large quantities because the print quality remains high.

Laser and Inkjet Their small size and low price have put these printers into many home offices as well as many businesses. The quality and the price are identified by the dots per inch (DPI). A higher DPI produces a crisper image but requires a higher price. Color images can also be printed on laser and inkjet printers. Desktop publishing has become a common practice for small businesses and home-based businesses. Almost anyone can produce a high-quality flyer or direct mail piece with this equipment.

CHECKPOINT

What is the most common printing method used?

____

____

THINK CRITICALLY

1. What is the relationship between the copy and the art?

2. What pattern do your eyes follow when you look at an advertisement?

3. What impression does your advertisement give if there is not enough white space?

4. Why is it important to proof your work before it is on the press?

5. What is relief printing?

MAKE CONNECTIONS

6. **RESEARCH** Use the library or Internet. How do laser and inkjet printers create an image on the paper? Write a description of the process, and compare it to one of the other print production processes.

7. **BUSINESS** Go to a local computer store, or use Internet suppliers. Identify a computer, a desktop publishing software package, and a high-quality printer. List, describe, and price the items. What is the total cost? What capabilities will the business owner gain from the equipment? Is it worth the cost? Be prepared to defend your decision.

8. **HISTORY** What was happening in the world at the time Gutenberg invented movable type? What was the impact of the invention? Write a one-page description of the surrounding events and the impact.

9. **ART** There are many principles of design in art. Using these principles will help you create and appreciate well-designed advertisements. Select one of the principles, such as balance or proportion. Write a definition, describe how it is used, and create an advertisement that illustrates the use of the principle.

LESSON 5.4
PUT THE AD ON TELEVISION

DEVELOP an effective storyboard

EXPLAIN the production process for a television advertisement

DEVELOP AN EFFECTIVE STORYBOARD

Television has been an incredible opportunity for advertisers. They have an audience that watches a series of five or six commercials until the main program returns.

Most people watch commercials. You cannot help yourself. You never know what you'll see, but it's bound to be interesting. Maybe lizards will chat casually with each other or a cow will dance. It might be someone just like you eating really good chocolate chip cookies, or there might be a sale on strawberries at the local grocery store. The medicine in the commercial might cure your itchy feet. Until you've seen a commercial once, it's difficult to look away.

ON THE $CENE

You are ready to design the television commercial for Ling Jen's jewelry stores. How will you take advantage of the visual element? How will you carry the advertising message from the print advertisement into the television commercial? What feature or benefit associated with her product and her custom design service will be the focus? How would you demonstrate her product?

ADVANTAGES OF TELEVISION ADVERTISING

Television advertising has many advantages built into the medium. The advantages make it irresistible to advertisers with money to spend.

- Almost every home in America has at least one television set. Most sets occupy a central location in the living room. Additional sets can often be found in bedrooms and the kitchen.
- A television program draws in a specific type of audience. Selecting the right time and channel to broadcast the commercial virtually guarantees that the target segment will be watching.
- Television has moving pictures. It seems like a simple concept, but the possibilities created by that statement are breathtaking to advertisers. You do not have to tell how good your product is. You can show it.
- The same people who are exposed to your commercial would never open their doors to strangers. Yet broadcasting a commercial is almost as good to the advertiser as having thousands of employees giving door-to-door demonstrations.
- Television is almost real to the audience. They become involved with the characters and the story lines in the programs they watch. Commercials with a continuing story line can build an audience's interest and trust.

DISADVANTAGES OF TELEVISION ADVERTISING

There are always a few disadvantages. Even an advertiser's dream medium has a few faults.

- Commercials are expensive to make, and airtime is expensive to buy. The better a time is for reaching consumers, the more the airtime will cost.
- The audience bores easily. As with most advertising media, you have about three seconds to catch viewers' interest.
- The audience bores quickly. The lifetime of a commercial is short. After viewers have seen a commercial several times, they begin to ignore it.

GUIDELINES

You should use an opening that grabs the audience's attention. If you do not get viewers' attention, they'll be reaching for the remote control. Try focusing the audience's attention on the visual components. The visual component is the advantage that television has over radio and print advertising. Also, coordinate the audio and visual elements. The copy and the images must support each other.

Most importantly, show the product. The product should be the focus of the commercial. Show close-ups of the product in action and the brand. Consumers will be more likely to remember the brand and recognize its appearance when they are shopping.

Select a familiar commercial. Draw the storyboard for the commercial. What events in the commercial would you put in the storyboard?

DEVELOP THE STORYBOARD

Television commercials require a storyboard. The **storyboard** is a series of sketches that show the sequential visual scenes and the matching copy for the commercial. The storyboard keeps track of the action and paces the action and text, ensuring a smooth flow of events in the commercial. Creating a storyboard is simple. Use graph paper or a graphic software application.

1. Draw a series of boxes, known as *frames.*
2. Sketch a scene in each frame. Use enough detail that it depicts where the elements and actors are when the copy is heard.
3. Write the words to any dialogue or voice-over below each frame.

When you are done, your storyboard will show the important moments in your commercial. The frames will look like a comic book version of the commercial. You are ready to begin the production phase of your commercial.

Does your dog seem a little listless lately?

Is he bored with his usual dog food?

Are his usual toys just not fun to him anymore?

It's time to bring your buddy to Pete's Pampered Pooch for an attitude adjustment!

We have great ideas for nutritious food and snacks, as well as row after row of fun, new toys!

Bring your buddy in today! He'll be glad you did!

CHECKPOINT

Why is it easy to locate the target segment for a commercial?

____

____

THE PRODUCTION PROCESS

Making a commercial is a process with many steps. The number of people and skills necessary to complete the project make the process complicated.

BEFORE PRODUCTION STARTS

A number of things have to be done before work can start on the commercial. Remember to consult the advertising plan.

Approve Storyboard and Script The written version of the storyboard is the script. The script is used to set the location, select actors, and set the budget. It also determines the schedule for making the commercial.

Approve Budget A general agreement about the budget was already documented in the advertising plan. The producer will estimate cost based on items such as location, actors, and staffing. The advertiser will have to approve this more specific budget.

Evaluate Possible Suppliers Selecting the director is one of the most critical decisions. The director makes many decisions that create the final look of your commercial. Businesses that supply editors and musicians have specific skills. You must select suppliers that meet your requirements.

Review Bids from Suppliers A production house is a business that provides individuals with technical skills, such as sound specialists and camera operators. Use the bid process to select providers with reasonable charges. The bid process ensures that you pay a reasonable rate for services. To receive a bid, select several companies that provide similar services, and send them the specifications of the job you want performed. The companies will submit bids that tell you how much they will charge for the service.

Create a Timetable Create a schedule for completing the commercial. It can be difficult to meet a production schedule, but you will have charges and expenses if you run over your schedule.

Select Location, Sets, and Cast Selecting your cast is the most important. The target segment must be able to identify with the actors. The actors have to match the product, the target segment, and the scene in the ad.

Pick Production submitted a bid for $600 per eight-hour day for a camera operator. Future Trends submitted a bid for $72.50 per hour. Compare the bids.

SOLUTION

Change the numbers to the same base units. Future Trends charges $72.50 per hour. How much is that per day?

Amount per hour × Hours in a day = Rate per day

$72.50 × 8 = Rate per day

$580.00 = Rate per day

Future Trends charges only $580 per day.

PRODUCTION

The shoot, or production phase of the commercial, is the most exciting and most stressful part of the process. On the first day, the director and lighting experts set up the lights and determine the time of day when the natural light is most predictable. If they film inside, natural light is not as critical. Correct lighting is one of the most important factors in creating a high-quality commercial. For this reason, the crew could spend an entire day setting up the lights correctly. The director walks the actors and the camera operators through the movements they will make during the commercial. This can prevent expensive mistakes later.

The director views the dailies every day during the production phase. *Dailies* are scenes shot the previous day. The director may see some reason to reshoot a scene (poor lighting, incorrect dialogue, or an inconsistency in quality). Even a hair out of place might be a reason to reshoot a scene.

Cost is a major reason for stress. Every problem that slows down production could extend the time required for shooting the commercial. If this happens, cost will go up as the number of people working additional time increases.

AFTER PRODUCTION

After the production phase is complete, several tasks remain. Experts with various skills are required. The postproduction work is also expensive.

When the director has accepted all the dailies, editing begins. Film editors piece together the best shots taken during a scene. The shots are known as *takes*. Each take may be just a little bit different. The camera may be at a different angle. The actor may have turned or smiled just a little bit more or less. A subtle difference can make one take perfect and another take flawed. The editing process combines different angles, close-ups, and wide shots to create the look you want.

The music is added to create a *rough cut*. A rough cut contains the best scenes edited together. The sound (including music, dialogue, and voice-overs) is in the rough cut. The rough cut is edited further until the final results are on-air quality, which is then suitable for broadcast.

What is the text version of the storyboard?

____

____

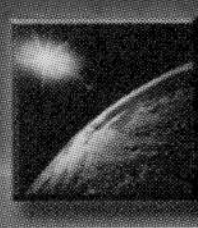

THINK CRITICALLY

1. Why do so many people see commercials?

2. Why is some airtime more expensive than other airtime?

3. Why do you focus attention on the visual element of the commercial?

4. What is a production house?

MAKE CONNECTIONS

5. **RESEARCH** Use the library or Internet. Sometimes a commercial requires a specific type of location, such as mountains or a lake. Select a geographic feature. Identify a location with that geographic feature. Write a one-page description of the location and how it could be used in the commercial.

6. **COMMUNICATION** Commercials often have dialogue. It can be difficult to write natural-sounding dialogue about a product. Write one page of dialogue that could be used in a commercial for toothpaste.

7. **PROBLEM SOLVING** You work for a director. It's your job, for this commercial, to locate a replica of the Statue of Liberty. What would you do?

8. **SOCIAL STUDIES** Use the library or Internet. Your agency has been asked to write a commercial about vacationing in America. The commercial will be viewed in another country. Select a country. Write a one-page summary of the current attitude the citizens have about vacationing in America. How would this affect your commercial?

REVIEW

CHAPTER SUMMARY

LESSON 5.1 Select a Strategy

A. An advertising message strategy identifies the advertiser's objectives and the methods used to carry out the objectives. Objectives can be based on the attributes of the product.

B. Objectives can be based on the attributes of the product's user. The slogan helps you remember a brand name.

LESSON 5.2 Write the Message

A. The creative plan contains information to create advertising for a client. Good advertising copy will follow the principles of good copywriting.

B. Each media form has strengths and weaknesses. It is important to apply the principles of good copywriting to writing for every medium.

LESSON 5.3 Put the Ad in Print

A. An effective advertisement uses the illustration and design to attract and keep viewers' attention, encouraging them to read the copy.

B. Desktop publishing revolutionized the print production process by creating tools everyone could use.

LESSON 5.4 Put the Ad on Television

A. An effective storyboard keeps track of the action and paces the action and text, ensuring a smooth flow of events in the commercial.

B. Making a commercial is a complicated process with many steps. A large number of people and skills are necessary to complete the project.

VOCABULARY BUILDER

Choose the term that best fits the definition. Write the letter of the answer in the space provided. Some terms may not be used.

____ **1.** Series of sketches that show the sequential visual scenes and the matching copy for a commercial

____ **2.** Short list of brand names you think of when a product or service is mentioned

____ **3.** Arrangement of elements in the advertisement

____ **4.** Catchphrase meant to help you remember a brand name

____ **5.** Paid placement on a web site

____ **6.** Advantage the consumer gets from a product feature

____ **7.** Drawing that shows where each element in the advertisement will be placed

____ **8.** Characteristic that is part of a product or service

____ **9.** Guideline to creating and constructing the advertising message

____ **10.** Everything in an advertisement that is not copy, including illustrations and design

a. art
b. banner ad
c. benefit
d. creative plan
e. design
f. evoked set
g. feature
h. layout
i. message strategy
j. slogan
k. storyboard

REVIEW CONCEPTS

11. What are some methods used to bring a brand name into a consumer's evoked set?

12. Why is humor in an advertisement risky?

13. What happens if the consumer's experience is transformed by the transformational strategy?

14. What is the purpose of the creative plan?

15. What is the negative approach in a headline?

16. What makes your advertisement different from one for your competition?

17. What are the components of an illustration?

18. What effect does the good use of white space produce?

b2000.swep.com

REVIEW

19. What are the stages in drawing a layout?

____

____

____

20. How long will a consumer pay attention to an advertisement that does not catch his or her attention?

____

____

____

21. Why does the advertiser have to approve a budget before production begins on a television commercial?

____

____

____

22. What characteristics should you look for when you select actors for a television commercial?

____

____

____

APPLY WHAT YOU LEARNED

23. Why is it important to study your client's product, company, and competition?

____

____

____

24. Are you interested in pursuing a career in producing television commercials? Why or why not?

____

____

____

25. Which message strategy is effective on you as a consumer? Explain.

____

____

____

26. Select a commercial you think is effective. Describe the characteristics of the commercial that make it effective.

27. Do you think computers will continue to impact the process of creating advertisements? Explain.

MAKE CONNECTIONS

28. HISTORY Identify and describe an early form of printing and distributing information.

29. PROBLEM SOLVING What aspects of the jewelry stores do you think Ling Jen should emphasize in the advertising campaign? Explain.

30. RESEARCH Use the Internet. Find banner advertisements on several web sites. Do they follow good copywriting principles? Explain.

31. SOCIAL STUDIES Use the Internet. Citizens of other countries can access web sites. Do you see any evidence that Internet advertisements have been internationalized? Explain and give examples.

32. BUSINESS MATH Pick Production submitted a bid for a film editor at $900 per eight-hour day. Future Trends submitted a bid for a film editor at $105 per hour. Which bid is the better deal for working an eight-hour day?

PLACE YOUR ADVERTISEMENT

LESSONS

6.1 DEVELOP THE MEDIA PLAN

6.2 USE SUPPORT MEDIA AND PROMOTIONS

6.3 DIRECT MARKETING AND PRESS RELEASES

CAREERS IN ADVERTISING

CLARKS COMPANIES

Clarks Companies, N.A., is a $300 million company that is a leader in the footwear industry. In the last four years, several of their brands have grown over 400 percent. The company has grown 200 percent in the same time period. The innovative footwear styles are manufactured in Franklin, WV. The distribution center in Hanover, PA, ships inventory to their 250+ retail stores and hundreds of wholesale customers.

The Retail Marketing Manager helps develop and execute promotional retail programs every month. Preparing and implementing the promotions for the grand opening of each new store is also part of the job. This manager supervises the creative process of visual presentation, maintains inventory levels at the retail sites, and ensures the smooth execution of wholesale marketing programs.

The position requires a college degree and three to five years experience in promotions or consumer marketing. Communication and computer skills are necessary. Travel is required.

THINK CRITICALLY

1. What appeals to you about the company and the position of Retail Marketing Manager?
2. Why are communication and computer skills required?

The Chapter 6 video for this module introduces the concepts in this chapter.

PROJECT

Advertising For Brookwood Department Store

PROJECT OBJECTIVES

- Develop a media plan to boost the store's poor performance
- Select support media to work with the media plan
- Design a P-O-P display or window display
- Write a press release

GETTING STARTED

Read through the Project Process below. Make a list of any materials you will need. Decide how you will get the needed materials or information.

- Brookwood Department Store has 25 retail locations in the tristate area. They employ over 2,000 workers at the retail sites and corporate office combined. Although the stores are profitable, their sales have dropped in the last three years. A new Chief Executive Officer, Oliver Thomas, will be joining the company next week. Hopefully, Mr. Thomas will be able to implement plans to make the store sales improve.
- Decide what information you need to gather for the project.
- Bring in promotional materials and news stories for related topics such as department stores and improving sales.
- Bring in materials for the P-O-P display or window display.

PROJECT PROCESS

Part 1 **LESSON 6.1** Select a message strategy and media plan that will be effective for the business. Choose a strategy to turn sales around.

Part 2 **LESSON 6.2** Design and create a P-O-P display or window display. Plan a sales promotion directed at the customer.

Part 3 **LESSON 6.3** Describe the role of public relations in turning the sagging sales around. Write a press release about Oliver Thomas becoming the new CEO.

CHAPTER REVIEW

Project Wrap-up Write the media plan. Build the P-O-P or window display. Use common objects to build an effective display. For example, if the window display requires mannequins, use dolls or have classmates pose in the display area. Write the press release about the new CEO, Oliver Thomas.

LESSON 6.1
DEVELOP THE MEDIA PLAN

IDENTIFY the components of a media plan

EVALUATE the media classes of newspaper, magazine, radio, and television

THE MEDIA PLAN

Selecting when and where to place your message is an important decision. You want to give the right message to the right people at the right time. If any of these conditions aren't met, you might as well not advertise at all.

Distributing your message in the media is the most expensive part of advertising. If you make the wrong choices, your advertising will be an expensive mistake. Therefore, it is important to make the right choices, to spend your advertising dollars wisely, and to earn money from your advertising.

Because your media choices are so critical, it is important to have a plan. A **media plan** identifies the media used to distribute an advertising message to the target audience. A good media plan will save money by selecting and buying the right exposure for your product. A media plan is driven by the advertising plan, and it is vital to the success of the creative plan. The media plan has four parts—media objectives, media strategies, media choices, and media scheduling and buying.

ON THE $CENE

Daniel Cruz is the Vice President of Marketing for a major company that manufactures products for domestic and foreign automobiles. The target segment is young men from 16 to 24 years old who repair their own cars or rebuild older cars as a hobby. The company also sells to owners of small auto-repair businesses. Daniel has been asked to approve the media plan for the coming year. How does he evaluate the plan? How does he judge the potential for success and the proposed schedule for advertising?

MEDIA OBJECTIVES

Objectives specify a media class and media vehicle. A **media class** is a type of media, such as television, radio, billboards, newspapers, or magazines. A **media vehicle** identifies a single member of the media class, such as *Good Housekeeping* or *Time*. Specific goals are necessary to make the media plan successful. Media objectives can be built around the five Ws—what, where, who, when, and why.

What The message to be delivered to the target segment is the result of the creative plan. It identifies the type of information to be delivered. This affects your media choices. For example, if your store is planning a large sale, you want to inform customers in a timely fashion. Newspaper, television, and radio can inform potential customers of the sale. Some media, such as billboards, would not be as effective.

Where One of the most important elements in setting objectives is the geographic coverage of the selected media. Advertisements placed in media outside of the geographic area where the product is sold would be a waste of money. For example, buying airtime on a Seattle radio station is worthless if the product is sold only in Phoenix. Media planners also can choose a geographic area to target with additional messages. Geotargeting can be used to reinforce purchasing tendencies that are already strong.

Who Reaching the target segment is another critical element in setting objectives. Match each medium's audience to the target segment. If the audience doesn't match the target segment, select a different medium rather than waste your advertising dollars.

When Media scheduling includes the message weight. **Message weight** identifies the number of times the audience is exposed to the advertising message by a specific media vehicle. Message weight includes duplication. In other words, if you see the ad twice while you are watching the same television show, it will count as two separate exposures.

Why The rationale directing the media campaign will provide reasons for making strategic media decisions. These decisions will determine the success or failure of the media plan.

MEDIA STRATEGY

The media objectives are the foundation of the media strategy. The media strategy determines the types of media that will be used, when and where the advertisements will run, and how often they will run. With the media objectives, two simple facts determine the media strategy.

1. Every day, the average consumer is exposed to more than 1,500 advertising messages.
2. People forget things, so they need to be reminded often.

The strategy must overcome these two facts. Repetition helps you remember. Ideally, a media plan would require a high level of advertising 52 weeks a year. Because this isn't financially possible, the advertiser has to make strategic choices.

Reach The percentage of the target audience that is exposed to an advertisement in the specified time period is the **reach**. If 20 percent of the advertiser's target segment reads the same weekly magazine, the magazine has a reach of 20 percent. **Frequency** is the number of times the audience is exposed to an advertisement in a specified time period. Analysts can't agree on the number of times a consumer should be exposed to an advertisement to make it effective. One exposure probably is not enough to affect the consumer's behavior. However, fewer exposures will be necessary for a simple message, while a complicated message will require more exposures.

Continuity Another strategic decision involves the pattern of placement in a media schedule. Advertisers can choose to run an ad at the same time or in the same media for a long period of time. It can also be effective to schedule two weeks of heavy advertising, take two weeks off, and then advertise heavily again. Finally, advertisers can combine the two methods by alternating heavy and light advertising.

Size The length of a broadcast ad or size of a print ad doesn't determine success. Decisions about length and size depend on the creative requirements and budget. If the cost of each ad is less because of size, it can be repeated more often while staying within the budget.

MEDIA CHOICES

The choice of media class is based on the objectives and strategy. Media planners can choose to use one medium, concentrating the media budget in a single medium. The planner can also select more than one media class, such as television and magazines. Choosing an assorted media mix enables an advertiser to place customized ads in different media classes and media vehicles to reach more than one target segment.

MEDIA SCHEDULING AND BUYING

All the planning and evaluation results in scheduling and buying advertising time or space. Final decisions are made to get the most impact from the time or space available in the chosen media vehicles and the budgeted funds.

Airtime or ad space can be purchased by the business, the ad agency, or an agency that specializes in buying and selling advertising time or space. The media-buying service makes money by purchasing large blocks of time or space in different media vehicles and reselling it to businesses.

Flexibility An effective media plan requires flexibility to address different events or situations. Changes in the market can create opportunities or pre-

The average cost of airtime for a 30-second television commercial during prime time is around $100,000. There is an average of 17 minutes of commercials during most hour-long shows during prime time. How much is the network earning during an average show?

SOLUTION

Multiply the number of minutes by 2 to get the number of 30-second spots.

$17 \times 2 = 34$

Multiply the number of 30-second spots by $100,000.

$34 \times \$100{,}000 = \$3{,}400{,}000$

The network earns $3,400,000 every hour for commercials.

sent threats. For example, difficulties for your competition can present your company with an opportunity. On the other hand, if your competition changes strategy, you may need to respond or increase the frequency of your advertisements. Changes in the media or media vehicles such as mergers or new media might require changes to your media choices or schedule.

CHECKPOINT

What is the difference between a media class and a media vehicle?

____

____

____

MEDIA CLASSES

Spending on advertising affects the business paying for the advertising and the consumers receiving the advertising messages. Spending on advertising also affects the media classes and vehicles carrying the advertisements. Combined, media vehicles earn billions of dollars. Print, radio, and television are the major media classes used by advertisers.

NEWSPAPERS

The advertising medium accessible to most businesses is the newspaper media class. National newspapers, such as *The Wall Street Journal*, reach a national audience. Local newspapers target a more precise geographic area, making them invaluable to local retailers. Some newspapers target specific audiences. For example, *The Wall Street Journal* targets the business segment.

Pros and Cons Newspapers offer several advantages to advertisers. First, newspapers reach over 50 percent of American homes. Newspapers are produced and delivered every day, which enables advertisers to respond quickly to competition or place timely ads for special events. Newspapers carry a reputation of credibility based on the news reports, which affects a reader's perception of the ads. The local focus of some sections provides an ideal location for local advertisers. Finally, the cost of creating and placing ads in a local newspaper is much lower than the cost of most media.

There are disadvantages as well. Consumers read the paper daily, but they also discard it daily. This short lifespan means businesses might do better if they place advertisements several times during the week. The newspaper may limit creative possibilities since ads may be limited to black and white.

Categories There are several kinds of ads. Display advertisements are located in the body area. They are usually set apart from the text by a border or white space. Inserts are printed on separate pages and folded into the newspaper. Sunday editions usually contain the most inserts. Small businesses as well as individuals can place classified ads.

Look through a magazine. How many advertisements are in the magazine? How do the advertisements take advantage of the media vehicle? How do they differ from newspaper ads?

MAGAZINES

Many magazines are published in the United States. Most magazines target consumers through sports, interests, or hobbies, or they target businesses through profession or industry.

Pros and Cons Advantages include the ability to target a specific segment, creative flexibility, and longer life than newspaper or broadcast messages. However, magazine advertising costs more than newspaper ads, requires lead times of two or more months, and offers only limited frequency.

Categories Advertisements can be full-page, half-page, two-column, one-column, or half-column. Ads also can have a bleed page, which occurs when the background runs to the edge of the page, eliminating the white space border. The gatefold ad folds out of the magazine to hold an extra-wide advertisement.

RADIO

Radio programming can be local or national. Your local station can be an affiliate of a national network, carrying only network programs. It could carry syndicated programs, or all the programming could be locally produced.

Pros and Cons Advantages include timeliness similar to newspaper ads, low cost, and the ability to reach consumers at home, at work, and in the car. On the negative side, listeners don't always pay attention to the background noise, and the audio-only environment is a creative challenge.

Categories Options include local spot advertising, network advertising, and national spot advertising in syndicated programs. The audience can be thousands or millions of listeners.

TELEVISION

The best advertising medium may be television. It offers sight and sound to stimulate a consumer to act.

Pros and Cons Television offers many advantages, including the ability to reach a specific target segment and to repeat the message frequently and the creative freedom to use a variety of effects to persuade the consumer. Television commercials have disadvantages as well. Commercials are so brief that repetition is necessary to affect a consumer. Commercials have a low credibility rating. Consumers just don't trust commercials as much as some other forms of advertising. Finally, audiences often reach for the remote control before the commercials even start during a program break.

Categories Options include local, syndicated, cable, and network. Local programming includes news and programs of interest to the community. Syndicated shows can be original or older network shows that are rebroadcast. Cable and network television transmit a variety of programs.

How can businesses reach a national audience with newspaper advertising?

____

____

THINK CRITICALLY

1. What are the four parts of a media plan?

2. What can you use to build the objectives for a media plan?

3. How does a business make decisions about the length or size of an ad?

4. Which advertising medium has the highest credibility rating? Explain.

5. What media require the least lead time?

MAKE CONNECTIONS

6. COMMUNICATION Compare an advertisement on the radio with an advertisement on television for the same product or a similar product. How does each advertisement take advantage of its medium? Write a one-page summary of your findings.

7. ART Compare the appearance of an advertisement in the newspaper with an advertisement in a magazine for the same product or a similar product. How does each advertisement take advantage of its medium? Prepare a presentation about your findings.

8. BUSINESS MATH Watch an hour of television. Count the number of minutes filled with commercials during the show. What is the ratio of commercial time to program time?

LESSON 6.2

USE SUPPORT MEDIA AND PROMOTIONS

DESCRIBE the techniques of using support media

EXPLAIN the role of sales promotion

USING SUPPORT MEDIA

Companies give away "freebies" all the time. Most items they give away are stamped with a name or logo identifying the company. These are also advertising tools.

Businesses are always looking for new places to advertise. They place signs on buses, give away pens, and buy uniforms for Little League teams. These are known as *support media.* They are used to reinforce a message delivered by a media vehicle.

SUPPORT MEDIA

Placing an advertising message near the *point-of-purchase* (P-O-P) is a valuable marketing practice. This can be done in a variety of ways.

Yellow Pages or Business Service Directories Businesses or individuals are ready to buy when they look in the phone book. Attract customers with a listing that displays more than a business name. This is particularly effective for small businesses.

ON THE $CENE

Daniel Cruz, the Vice President of Marketing for a manufacturer of products for domestic and foreign automobiles, is analyzing the media plan for the coming year. He is concerned that the plan doesn't include any support media and the planned sales promotions don't seem to be effective for the target segment. What should he suggest to the department that prepared the plan?

Outdoor Advertising Signs on your building inform customers of your business location 24 hours a day, attracting local customers. Billboards use color, lighting, and special effects to create a unique image of your product or business. Outdoor advertising can be placed on almost any object that is outside, including walls, benches, and vehicles.

Transit advertising includes signs located on buses, trains, and subways, as well as posters in the stations for these transit systems. Transit advertising is aimed at travelers and regular commuters.

Point-of-Purchase Displays Consumer decisions are affected by displays or signs located in the store near the items to be purchased. P-O-P displays can include signs, banners, and special display racks. Effective P-O-P displays are located in high-traffic areas at a height where customers will notice the display and identify the product.

By creating an atmosphere and an interest in a product, window displays are very effective at enticing customers to enter the store. These displays enable you to visually promote a product. Change window displays frequently to create interest for people who would normally pass by without entering.

Sponsorship Businesses can choose to sponsor international, national, or local events or participants in events. **Event sponsorship** occurs when a business helps to fund an event in exchange for displaying a brand name, logo, or advertising message at the event, in any literature about the event, or during any broadcasts of the event. Events can include the international Olympic Games or a local craft show held in the park each summer.

Businesses can also sponsor individuals or teams in some events. In NASCAR racing, for example, businesses will often sponsor a single racing team. This means that the business will help to pay the team's expenses in exchange for displaying the company's logo or product name on the car and the team uniforms. For the entire race, viewers in the stands and the television audience watch the car (and the company's advertising message) drive around the track.

Smaller businesses often sponsor local events or teams. A local bank or restaurant can sponsor a children's soccer league by purchasing uniforms for the teams in exchange for displaying a business logo on the uniforms.

Sponsorship can benefit the business, the event or team, and the community. Businesses gain prestige, improve their public image, and receive advertising opportunities. Events or teams benefit by receiving funds that enable them to hold the event or participate in the event. Communities benefit by gaining visitors for the event and increasing the satisfaction of its citizens.

did you KNOW?

Revenue from outdoor advertising is growing 10 percent each year. Advertisers spent more than $4.8 billion on outdoor advertising in 1999. More facts about outdoor advertising can be found at the web site for the Outdoor Advertising Association of America, Inc., at www.oaaa.org.

CHECKPOINT

What is P-O-P advertising?

____

____

THE ROLE OF SALES PROMOTION

Sometimes advertising doesn't seem like an advertisement. If you have ever entered a contest or sweepstakes sponsored by a company, you have responded to a sales promotion. **Sales promotion** is the use of incentives to increase the brand value for consumers or distributors. Promotions are aimed at customers or distributors.

PROMOTIONS FOR CONSUMERS

Sales promotion doesn't have the same effect as advertising. Sales promotion is meant to cause an immediate purchase rather than a long-term change in consumer behavior. Of course, increasing sales for a short time can result in long-term increases as well.

Methods Techniques such as coupons, contests, and rebates encourage consumers to buy specific products. Most methods work best with a specific objective.

- ***Coupons*** A reduction in price for a buyer is provided by a coupon. Coupons might cause a consumer to change brand loyalties or buy a product again.
- ***Premiums*** Items that are free or cost less with the purchase of another item are premiums. Cold cereals frequently use this tactic to encourage purchases.
- ***Contests*** When consumers use a skill to compete for a prize, they participate in a contest. Contests can be expensive to administer because each entry must be judged.
- ***Sweepstakes*** When winners are determined by chance, consumers have entered a sweepstakes.
- ***Sampling*** Many grocery stores offer small samples of food products. The samples are intended to persuade consumers to buy the products.

GROCERY COUPONS Catalina Marketing Corp. combined the technology of the Universal Product Code (UPC) with a new marketing strategy to build a business worth $172 million in 1998. In 1983, scanners were used by most large grocery stores. The information collected by the scanners was used to track inventory and speed up the checkout process. Catalina used the UPC information to print coupons for products the consumer actually bought. This type of targeting set new standards. In the first week of testing, sales affected by the coupons increased 60 percent and the 8–14 percent coupon redemption rate far surpassed the 1–2 percent achieved by previous methods.

THINK CRITICALLY Why did this method increase sales so drastically? What other methods are used to distribute coupons? How does Catalina earn money?

- ***Rebates*** This money-back offer is from the manufacturer to the consumer. The retailer where the consumer bought the item is not involved.
- ***Frequency*** Regular buyers are rewarded with special deals or offers.

Objectives Set specific objectives for a sales promotion. This will determine the methods that will be most effective.

- ***Trial Purchase*** New users can be enticed into buying a new product by coupons or rebates.
- ***Repeat Purchase*** Coupons in the package and rewards for frequent buyers can persuade buyers to purchase the product again.
- ***Buy Larger Amounts*** Price reductions, sales, and packaging larger quantities together persuade consumers to buy more, which reduces inventory and increases cash flow for the business.
- ***New Brand*** Promotions can encourage consumers to buy new products.

Examine your local Sunday newspaper. What types of consumer promotions are advertised in the newspaper? Which methods are most effective?

PROMOTIONS FOR DISTRIBUTORS

Businesses offer promotions to distributors, including wholesalers and retailers, as well. Promotions can interest distributors in a product and create enthusiasm about selling the product. Running a promotion for distributors at the same time as a consumer promotion may ensure the distributors' cooperation.

Methods Just as there are techniques to encourage consumers to buy products, there are methods to encourage distributors to buy more products. Distributors will sell those products to consumers.

- ***P-O-P Displays*** Retailers want displays that will sell the product.
- ***Incentives*** Rewards for reaching specific sales goals are very effective.
- ***Cooperative Advertising*** Free product advertising provides space for the retailer to insert its name.

Objectives Well-defined objectives lead to success. Methods can be matched to the objectives.

- ***Begin Distribution of New Product*** Incentives encourage distributors to provide shelf space for new products.
- ***Encourage Larger Orders*** Incentives can persuade distributors to maintain more inventory at their sites. This lowers costs for the manufacturer.
- ***Encourage Distributor to Work with Promotions for Consumers*** Distributors may need to maintain larger inventories or provide special displays.

Who is the target of sales promotion?

____

____

THINK CRITICALLY

1. Why is it so effective to place a larger display listing in the phone book?

2. What do businesses gain from sponsoring an event?

3. What is the effect of window displays?

4. How does a sales promotion differ from an advertisement?

5. What is the difference between a contest and a sweepstakes?

MAKE CONNECTIONS

6. **RESEARCH** Use the Internet or library. Which companies sponsored the most recent Olympics? Did the sponsorship impact the companies' revenues? Describe your findings in a one-page summary.
7. **COMMUNICATION** Brand placement is an interesting advertising method that involves the use of branded products in movies. The next time you watch a movie, make a list of the brands that appear in the movie. Write a one-page description of the products used.

8. **COMMUNICATION** Suppose you work for a manufacturer. Write a letter to a retailer that explains a sales promotion for distributors and customers that will occur at the same time. Be sure to explain the benefits to the retailer.

LESSON 6.3

DIRECT MARKETING AND PRESS RELEASES

EXPLAIN the growth of direct marketing

WRITE a press release

DIRECT MARKETING

How much attention do you pay to a message directed specifically to you? Most people pay more attention to something directed to them than to an advertisement placed in the media. This is the theory behind direct marketing. **Direct marketing** is an interactive method of marketing designed to generate a measurable response or transaction. Direct marketing is intended to close a sale, identify prospects for future contacts, or reinforce a customer's brand loyalty. Direct marketing can include direct mail, but it also includes methods such as telemarketing and magazine inserts.

GROWTH OF DIRECT MARKETING

In 1998, 180 million people purchased products as a result of direct marketing. The United States has a $1.5 trillion market for direct marketing. The market is growing 8.6 percent every year. For example, over 10,000 different catalogs are currently mailed in the United States.

ON THE $CENE

Daniel Cruz, the Vice President of Marketing for a manufacturer of products for domestic and foreign automobiles, is analyzing the media plan for the coming year. He notices that a direct marketing campaign is planned. It includes a direct mail package and inserts in a popular magazine for mechanics. Would you recommend any additions or modifications to the plan?

Advances in technology are responsible for this growth. Computers enable a business to collect and keep huge amounts of information. Credit cards have made it easy for consumers to buy without going into the store.

MAILING LISTS AND DATABASES

The one element that might determine the success or failure of your direct marketing effort is the quality of your mailing list or database. The right list will provide much better results than a random list of names. The best list to start with is a list of your own customers. It is easier to sell to customers familiar with your company and your products than to sell to other individuals. In the United States, databases and mailing lists are considered to be property. Therefore, theft or misuse is a crime.

Mailing List A list of consumers can be rented from a list broker, who can provide a compiled list or a response list. A compiled list contains individuals with shared characteristics such as occupation, age, or income. It is less expensive and less effective than a response list. A response list contains individuals who have shown an interest in a specific field. The list is more expensive than a compiled list but is more effective because it identifies people who are already interested in your product. Often response lists are rented with the restriction that the list owner must approve the content of your direct mail package.

Database A large collection of data organized for easy search and retrieval is a database. The database separates direct marketing from any other type of marketing or advertising. The information in a mailing list can be kept in a database. However, a database can contain much more information that provides a clear picture of the potential customer. Hobbies, health, education level, value of your house, previous purchases, and level of debt are just a small sample of the information that could be stored in a database.

DIRECT MAIL

The traditional direct mail package has four printed components. The letter informs the consumer of the benefits of the product and urges the reader to respond. The brochure or data sheet describes the product features and

ADVERTISING GLOBALLY

International direct marketing is proving to be very successful. American technology, including computer hardware and software, is very popular in many other countries. Because in many countries sources are limited and demand is high, profits can be significant. A list broker provides mailing lists for different countries. Before sending any mailings, American export companies must investigate mailing and shipping regulations for the country. Shipping to a foreign country is often more difficult than selling.

THINK CRITICALLY What American products are popular in other countries?

benefits. The reply vehicle tells the reader how to respond to the package, such as calling or sending the order form. The envelope the direct mail package arrives in usually has a *teaser*, some text that will interest the consumer in opening the package.

Letter The most important piece in the direct mail package is the letter. It should contain a compelling description of the product benefits. The body of the letter should repeatedly urge the reader to respond. Although the letter is really a long advertisement, it should look like a letter. This lends more credibility and creates a more personal relationship with the reader.

Address the letter to the target segment. For example, "Dear Gardener" or "Dear Artist" defines the segment and identifies the reader's area of interest met by the product. Use your best benefits first to hold the reader's attention. Graphics also help to hold interest. Use short sentences and short paragraphs. Include a PS at the end. Almost every reader will read the PS.

Work with a partner. Select a familiar product. Write a letter to include in a direct mail package selling the product. What benefits of the product would you include in the letter?

E-MAIL MARKETING

Direct marketing recently began including e-mail as a tool. Studies have shown that e-mail, with an embedded web site address for the business, has a response rate higher than the traditional direct marketing tool of postal mail. The ease of simply clicking to view the business web site is probably an important factor in the response rate. E-mail that looks like a web page, using graphics and different kinds of type, gets an even higher response rate.

TELEMARKETING

Telemarketing, a major type of direct marketing, accounts for $460 billion in sales and employs 8.7 million people. Telemarketing is clearly successful, but many consumers consider it intrusive. In the past few years, the use of computers to dial phone numbers has concerned many consumers who don't want to be contacted by telemarketers. By federal law, telemarketers can call consumers only between 8 a.m. and 9 p.m. They also must remove the individual's name from the list, if requested.

OTHER METHODS

The small postcard inserts in magazines are another form of direct marketing. In addition to calling your attention to a product, the insert usually asks for some type of personal information, such as income or occupation, or information about your behavior as a consumer. Depending on the topic, they might ask if you own a specific item or if you intend to buy one.

Infomercials are also a type of direct marketing. Several times during the commercial, you are asked to call or contact the company for more information or to purchase the item.

What is the purpose of direct marketing?

WRITING A PRESS RELEASE

A company handles news about itself by controlling the release of company information as much as possible. The most important tool your company can use to communicate with the media is the press release. A **press release** is a statement prepared for distribution to the media that provides information that is timely, accurate, and interesting. Often the press release is your first contact with the media about a specific event at your company. The press release should fill a purpose.

- ***Announce a significant event for your company.*** Significant events include winning an award, sponsoring an event, opening a new office, hiring or promoting corporate officers, and introducing a new product.
- ***Interest the media in writing about your product or company.*** Although you may be tempted to call the media when an event occurs, the press release is the method of contact preferred by the media.
- ***Create awareness of your company or your product.*** Depending on the level of media coverage generated by your press release, thousands or millions of people could be exposed to your company or your product.

The level of press coverage generated by a press release is based partly on the potential impact on the audience. For example, if you own one sandwich shop that employs 15 part-time workers and you open a second sandwich shop on the other side of town, your press release will generate some local coverage. If you are a major U.S. software company that employs thousands of workers and you open another office in a different state or a different country, your press release will generate national or international news.

PUBLIC RELATIONS

Public relations is the business function that works with the media. Because public relations includes the company's public image, it is also a marketing function.

Public Image Improving and maintaining the company's public image is an important part of public relations. This includes telling about good deeds performed by the company or the company's employees. For example, the company could donate computers to a local school or help a community struck by a natural disaster. Employees might donate time to an adult literacy project or spend weekends helping to build housing for low-income families. Preventing negative events from damaging the company's image is also a public relations function. A worker injured on the job can lead to negative information or rumors of poor safety practices. An employee involved in an auto accident while driving a company vehicle can open the door to all kinds of negative stories in the media.

Product Announcements Product announcements made by the public relations department can also be newsworthy. The medical field often makes product announcements. Sometimes thousands of people can be affected by a single medical breakthrough or a new medication. Of course,

Select a commercial for a medical product. Based on the information in the commercial, list some statements that may have appeared in the product announcement. Explain your list to the class.

every product announcement won't be on the evening news. While a new toy for dogs may make millions of dogs happy, it does not have the same impact on the audience viewing the news as advances in treatment for cancer.

Structure and Format Every press release should follow the same structure and format so media people receiving your press release can easily find the information. Try to limit the press release to two pages.

- ***For Immediate Release*** Use paper with a letterhead. Key the words "FOR IMMEDIATE RELEASE" under the letterhead. Make it bold in all capital letters, and use a font size that is larger than the remaining text.
- ***Contact Information*** Leave one or two blank lines after the release statement. Enter the name, title, telephone and fax numbers, and e-mail address of the person in your company who can be contacted for more information. Include a home phone number. Journalists may need to make contact in the evening if a deadline is approaching.

Blue Butterfly Garden
143 First Avenue
Smallville, Ohio 45042
(513) 555-1298

FOR IMMEDIATE RELEASE

Mitch Kleener
Public Information Officer
Office: (513) 555-1298
Home: (513) 555-7639
Fax: (513) 555-1297

Blue Butterfly Garden Grows

Smallville—May 1, 2001: Blue Butterfly Garden, the nation's largest supplier of plants and gardening equipment, has acquired Giller's. Giller's is a leading catalog service located in Dayton, Ohio.

Wayne Bend, chief operating officer of Blue Butterfly Garden, announced the acquisition on May 1, 2001. "We are very excited about the opportunity this presents to our customers. This acquisition will enable us to add catalog sales to our customer service offerings. In the next six months, we will also add an Internet site that provides gardening information and landscape plans, as well as the convenience of placing orders online."

The acquisition will add 68 employees to Blue Butterfly Garden's personnel. Bend added, "No jobs will be lost. In fact, we plan to increase our staff to meet the additional demand we expect from catalog and Internet sales."

Bend concluded, "This acquisition is good for us and for our customers. As we grow, our customers will receive a wider variety of services delivered with the same Blue Butterfly Garden's standard of quality."

# # #

- ***Headline*** Leave one or two blank lines after the contact information. Key the headline. Make it bold.
- ***Dateline*** Enter the city where the press release originated and the date the press release was mailed. Begin your first paragraph on the same line.
- ***Lead Paragraph*** Start on the same line as the date.
- ***Body*** Key the main text of the press release. At the bottom of each page, except the last page, key "-more-" centered alone on the last line.
- ***Conclusion*** Restate the important information in the press release. At the end of the article, key "###" or "30" centered on a line by itself to indicate the end of the article.

Content The headline, lead paragraph, and body contain the information. Each section fulfills a purpose in the press release.

The *headline* must attract the reader's attention. Keep it short, never more than a sentence in length.

The *lead paragraph* is critical. Readers will either stop here or read most of the press release. Set the tone. Fit in as much critical information as possible. Use the journalist's five Ws—what, where, who, when, and why. Keep the pace lively. Don't get bogged down in specifics in the first paragraph.

The *body* contains the details. Use quotes and bulleted lists wherever possible. This will break up any long blocks of text and highlight critical information. Quotes enable you to insert opinions into the article. You can quote someone else saying your product is a good one.

- ***Make sure your facts are accurate.*** Never give information to the media that hasn't been checked. They will find your mistakes.
- ***Use a factual, journalistic approach.*** Put key information first. Don't include personal opinions. Use the third person. Describe "the company," not "my company." Refer to yourself by name, not as "I" or "me."
- ***Write in a simple and straightforward manner.*** Use brief sentences. Avoid flowery phrases.
- ***Keep the most important information near the top.*** Readers won't miss any critical details if they stop at the halfway point.

Distribution A press release is intended to provide information for journalists. Whether the media ever uses the press release, it can be an effective marketing tool. You can distribute a press release at a trade show or speaking engagement, mail it to associations related to your industry, or include it in a direct mailing package.

What determines the level of press coverage given to a press release?

____

____

THINK CRITICALLY

1. What is responsible for the growth of direct marketing? Explain.

2. What is a list broker?

3. Why should the letter in the direct mail package look like a letter?

4. What is publicity?

5. What are the journalist's five Ws?

MAKE CONNECTIONS

6. **RESEARCH** Use the Internet. The National Mail Order Association (NMOA) maintains a web site at www.nmoa.org. Write a one-page description of the information on the site that could help you prepare the direct marketing portion of an advertising campaign.

7. **GOVERNMENT** Use the library or Internet. Investigate the Telephone Consumer Protection Act (TCPA) passed in 1991. Why was this act passed? Write a one-page description of the effects on direct marketing.

8. **JOURNALISM** Read several articles in the business section of your newspaper. Which articles probably resulted from a press release? Write a one-page description of the event that triggered the press release.

REVIEW

CHAPTER SUMMARY

LESSON 6.1 Develop the Media Plan

A. The components of a media plan are media objectives, media strategies, media choices, and media scheduling and buying. Reach, continuity, and size play an important role in effective media strategies.

B. The media classes of newspaper, magazine, radio, and television have advantages and disadvantages that make each one unique. While newspapers have a greater reach, they are often discarded daily. Television offers sight and sound to stimulate consumers to act.

LESSON 6.2 Use Support Media and Promotions

A. Support media, such as outdoor advertising, point-of-purchase displays, and event sponsorship, are used to reinforce a message delivered by a media vehicle.

B. Sales promotion is meant to cause an immediate purchase using incentives such as coupons, rebates, sweepstakes, and sampling.

LESSON 6.3 Direct Marketing and Press Releases

A. The growth of direct marketing is the result of advances in technology. The quality of a mailing list or database will also affect marketing success.

B. Public relations controls a company's public image. The press release, a public relations tool, has a standard structure and format. Most companies provide press releases to the media.

VOCABULARY BUILDER

Choose the term that best fits the definition. Write the letter of the answer in the space provided. Some terms may not be used.

____ **1.** Statement prepared for distribution to the media

____ **2.** Percentage of the target audience that is exposed to an advertisement in the specified time period

____ **3.** Number of times the audience is exposed to the advertising message

____ **4.** Use of incentives to increase the brand value for consumers or distributors

____ **5.** When a business helps to fund an event in exchange for displaying a brand name, logo, or advertising message

____ **6.** Type of media, such as television or magazines

____ **7.** Number of times the audience is exposed to an advertisement in a specified time period

____ **8.** Identifies the media used to distribute an advertising message to the target audience

____ **9.** Interactive method of marketing designed to generate a measurable response or transaction

a. direct marketing
b. event sponsorship
c. frequency
d. media class
e. media plan
f. media vehicle
g. message weight
h. press release
i. reach
j. sales promotion

REVIEW CONCEPTS

10. What is the purpose of media strategy?

11. Why is it important to be flexible in a media plan?

12. Which media classes are used most often by advertisers?

13. What is transit advertising, and who is the target?

14. Who benefits when a company sponsors an event or a team?

15. What promotional methods target customers?

16. What promotional methods target distributors?

17. What separates direct marketing from any other type of advertising?

18. What part of the direct mail package do most people read?

19. What three purposes does the press release fill?

APPLY WHAT YOU LEARNED

20. Explain the relationship between the advertising plan, the media plan, and the creative plan.

21. What local events or teams could a business sponsor?

22. Describe the most memorable outdoor advertising you pass regularly. Why is it memorable?

23. Read the business section of your newspaper. What events have occurred recently for local companies?

24. What is your opinion about companies maintaining and selling databases filled with customer information? Explain.

MAKE CONNECTIONS

25. BUSINESS MATH Contact a local radio station. Compare the prices the station charges for advertising at different times during the day. Make a spreadsheet showing this information. What time is the best buy, taking into account the number of listeners at the time?

26. PROBLEM SOLVING Suppose you are a media planner. What media vehicles should a local restaurant use to target consumers your age? What media vehicles would reach your parents? Is there any overlap? Explain.

____

____

27. ART Examine a P-O-P display in a local store. What makes it effective?

____

____

28. SOCIAL STUDIES Use the library or Internet. Identify a country interested in buying American products. What characteristics of the country or the population would make this country a good candidate for direct marketing? Explain.

____

____

29. GOVERNMENT Use the library or Internet. Investigate the *Deceptive Mail Prevention and Enforcement Act* that became law on December 12, 1999, and took effect on April 12, 2000. Write a one-page summary of the law.

30. COMMUNICATION Write the lead paragraph of a press release announcing the promotion of Phil Stroud to senior vice president.

____

____

____

31. PROBLEM SOLVING Contact a local media vehicle. Request a media kit. List the information in the kit, and explain its importance.

____

____

____

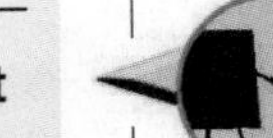

32. PROBLEM SOLVING Suppose you work in the marketing department of a major cookie producer. Create a special promotion for customers.

GLOSSARY

A

Advertisement paid public announcement persuading you to buy an item or a service (p. 7)

Advertising agency company made up of professionals who specialize in providing creative and business services involved in planning, preparing, and placing advertisements (p. 36)

Advertising plan the thinking and tasks needed to achieve a successful advertising campaign that fits into the advertiser's marketing strategy (p. 81)

Advertising research the thorough investigation of the planning, preparation, and placement of advertisements (p. 69)

Art everything in the advertisement that is not copy, including the illustration and design (p. 118)

B

Banner ad paid advertising on a web site (p. 116)

Benefit the advantage the consumer gets from a feature (p. 112)

C

Coincidental studies measurement tools that provide real-time information about the campaign's impact (p. 95)

Community a group of people with a common characteristic or interest living within a larger society (p. 58)

Competitor analysis part of the advertising plan that examines the identity, strengths, and weaknesses of the competition and competing product (p. 83)

Consumer someone who uses products (p. 4)

Consumer behavior everything that affects or is affected by human consumption (p. 5)

Creative boutique specializes in developing creative concepts, writing creative text, and providing artistic services (p. 41)

Creative plan guideline to creating and constructing the advertising message that coordinates the copywriting, art, and media (p. 111)

Culture integrated pattern of behavior, knowledge, and beliefs that are acquired from a group and passed on to future generations (p. 57)

D

Demographics statistical characteristics of human populations such as age, race, gender, income, marital status, education, and occupation (p. 63)

Design the arrangement of elements in the advertisement (p. 120)

Direct marketing an interactive method of marketing designed to generate a measurable response or transaction (p. 147)

E

Event sponsorship a business helps to fund an event in exchange for displaying a brand name, logo, or advertising message at the event, in literature about the event, or in broadcasts of the event (p. 143)

Evoked set a short list of brand names you think of when a product or service is mentioned (p. 105)

Executive summary part of the advertising plan that provides a summary of the most important information needed to make decisions (p. 82)

External facilitators perform specialized services for advertisers and advertising agencies (p. 36)

F

Feature a characteristic that is part of a product or service (p. 112)

Focus group a group of six to twelve consumers, led by a professional moderator, who discuss the product (p. 72)

Frequency the number of times the audience is exposed to an advertisement in a specified time period (p. 137)

Full-service agency provides a wide range of services designed to meet a client's complete advertising needs (p. 41)

I

Industry a distinct group of productive or profit-making businesses (p. 34)

Industry analysis part of the advertising plan that examines industry developments and trends in (p. 83)

In-house agency advertising department in a company whose main business is not advertising (p. 41)

Interactive agencies specialize in helping clients prepare advertising for new interactive media, such as Internet, CD-ROMs, and interactive television (p. 41)

L

Layout a drawing that shows where each element in the advertisement will be placed (p. 120)

M

Market analysis part of the advertising plan that examines customers and their motives for buying the product (p. 83)

Market segment a group of people that have common characteristics and similar needs and wants (p. 63)

Marketing mix all marketing activities, such as advertising, sales promotions, event sponsorships, and public relations (p. 38)

Mass media a form of communication designed to reach a large number of people (p. 14)

Media-buying service an organization that specializes in buying media time and space, particularly on radio and television stations (p. 41)

Media class a type of media, such as television, radio, billboards, newspapers, or magazines (p. 137)

Media plan identifies the media used to distribute an advertising message to the target audience (p. 136)

Media vehicle single member of a media class, such as *Good Housekeeping* magazine (p. 137)

Message strategy part of the advertising plan that includes the advertiser's objectives and methods used to carry out the objectives (p. 104)

Message weight the number of times the audience is exposed to the advertising message by a specific media vehicle (p. 137)

N

Need something you can't live without, such as food, clothes, and shelter (p. 4)

O

Overview part of the advertising plan that identifies the document's structure and the material that will be covered in the plan (p. 82)

P

Positioning the process of making an advertiser's product different from other products in the consumer's mind (pp. 66, 93)

Press release statement prepared for distribution to the media that provides information that is timely, accurate, and interesting (p. 150)

Puffery the use of superlatives such as "greatest," "best," or "number one" (p. 48)

R

Reach percentage of the target audience that is exposed to an advertisement in the specified time period (p. 137)

Return on investment the amount you earn from the money you spend (p. 94)

Ritual formalized act or series of acts performed frequently (p. 57)

S

Sales promotion the use of incentives to increase the brand value for consumers or distributors (p. 144)

Search time the amount of time you would spend to find products or services you want (p. 12)

Situational analysis part of the advertising plan that examines the conditions and circumstances that affect the product or service (p. 82)

Slogan catchphrase meant to help you remember a brand name (p. 105)

Social class a group sharing the same economic or social status (p. 57)

Social meaning the interpretation of a product or service in a social context (p. 20)

Society a community, group, or large grouping of people with common traditions, institutions, activities, and interests (p. 12)

Standard of living the minimum level of necessities and luxuries required to maintain an individual or a group at a common level of comfort (p. 13)

Storyboard a series of sketches that show the sequential visual scenes and the matching copy for a television commercial (p. 126)

T

Target segment a subgroup of the market that is chosen to be the focus of the marketing and advertising campaign (p. 62)

Top-of-the-mind awareness test that identifies the leading brands in a specific product category by asking the consumer to name the brands in that category (p. 87)

W

Want something you would like to have but can live without (p. 5)

INDEX

U

V

W

Y

PHOTO CREDITS

CHAPTER 1 4, 5, 10, 12, 13, 17, 19 © PhotoDisc; 14 © Eyewire; 16 © Corbis

CHAPTER 2 28 © Corbis; 29, 31, 32, 34, 37, 40, 42, 45, 48 © PhotoDisc

CHAPTER 3 56, 57, 59, 60, 62, 65, 66, 69, 70 © PhotoDisc

CHAPTER 4 80, 82, 84, 86, 87, 92, 93, 94, 96 © PhotoDisc; 89 © Eyewire

CHAPTER 5 104, 118, 120, 121 © Corbis; 106, 107, 109, 111, 113, 114, 115, 116, 122, 124, 125, 128 © PhotoDisc

CHAPTER 6 136, 139, 142, 143, 147 © Corbis; 144, 149 © PhotoDisc